Brown Skin, White Masks

T0327255

BROWN SKIN, WHITE MASKS

Hamid Dabashi

Fernwood Publishing
HALIFAX & WINNIPEG
www.fernwoodpublishing.ca

First published 2011 by Pluto Press
345 Archway Road, London N6 5AA
www.plutobooks.com

Published in Canada by Fernwood Publishing
32 Oceanvista Lane, Black Point, Nova Scotia, B0J 1B0
and 748 Broadway Avenue, Winnipeg, MB R3G 0X3
www.fernwoodpublishing.ca

Fernwood Publishing Company Limited gratefully acknowledges the financial
support of the Government of Canada through the Canada Book Fund, the Canada
Council for the Arts, the Nova Scotia Department of Tourism and Culture and the
Province of Manitoba, through the Book Publishing Tax Credit, for our publishing
program.

Library and Archives Canada Cataloguing in Publication
Dabashi, Hamid, 1951–

Brown skin, white masks / Hamid Dabashi.
Includes bibliographical references and index.
ISBN 978–1–55266–424–7
    1. Muslims—Violence against. 2. Muslims—Social conditions—21st century.
3. United States—History, Military—21st century. 4. Islamophobia—United States.
I. Title.
BP52.D32 2011   305.6'97
C2010-906377-5

Copyright © Hamid Dabashi 2011

The right of Hamid Dabashi to be identified as the author of this work has been
asserted by him in accordance with the Copyright, Designs and Patents Act 1988.

British Library Cataloguing in Publication Data
A catalogue record for this book is available from the British Library

ISBN   978 0 7453 2874 4   Hardback
ISBN   978 0 7453 2873 7   Paperback (Pluto)
ISBN   978 1 55266 424 7   Paperback (Fernwood)
ISBN   978 1 8496 4573 7   PDF eBook
ISBN   978 1 7837 1394 3   EPUB eBook
ISBN   978 1 7837 1395 0   Kindle eBook

Library of Congress Cataloging in Publication Data applied for

10   9   8   7   6   5   4   3   2   1

Designed and produced for Pluto Press by
Chase Publishing Services Ltd, 33 Livonia Road, Sidmouth, EX10 9JB, England
Typeset from disk by Stanford DTP Services, Northampton, England

In memory of:

Abeer Qassim Hamza al-Janabi (1991–2006)
The 14-year old Iraqi girl who was gang-raped and murdered
by the US Marines on March 12, 2006.

...and in hope of a future full of love and peace for

Moshe Holtzberg
The two-year old Jewish boy whose parents Rabbi Gavriel
Holtzberg and Rivka Holtzberg were murdered by militant
Muslims in Mumbai on November 27, 2008.

Contents

Why am I writing this book? Nobody asked me to. Especially not those for whom it is intended.

Frantz Fanon (1952)

Introduction
Informing Empires

I really do believe we will be greeted as liberators...I've talked with a lot of Iraqis in the last several months myself, had them to the White House.
> —US Vice President Dick Cheney to ABC Newscaster
> Tim Russert, September 14, 2003

A QUESTIONER: Vice President Cheney yesterday said that he expects that American forces will be greeted as liberators and I wonder if you could tell us if you agree with that and how you think they'll be greeted...?

KANAN MAKIYA: I most certainly do agree with that. As I told the President on January 10, I think they will be greeted with sweets and flowers in the first months and simply have very, very little doubts that that is the case.
> —Kanan Makiya, an Iraqi academic living in exile in the US.
> Said at the National Press Club, Washington, DC, September 15, 2003

In November 2008, the front pages of newspapers around the globe featured dramatic headlines about, and frightening pictures of, senseless acts of violence in Mumbai, India, where a band of militant adventurers went on a rampage in a number of heavily populated public spaces: a railway station, a popular café, a Jewish outreach center, a hospital, and two luxury hotels.[1] At least 173 people were murdered and many more were wounded. India, as usual, accused Pakistan; Pakistan denied any involvement.[2]

The mayhem in India marred the Thanksgiving holiday in the United States. Within hours of the shooting, the victims of the attack had been identified and CNN and other North American and European networks were giving details of their lives and their deaths. Here was a snapshot of Kia Sherr with her husband, Alan, and their daughter, Naomi, who, she told CNN, had both been killed in Mumbai. Here was a story about Rabbi Gavriel Noah Holtzberg, 29, and his wife Rivka, 28, of the Chabad-Lubavitch, who were killed inside the Nariman House. Their toddler, Moshe, had been carried out to safety by his nanny, Sandra Samuel, and was now safe with his grandparents in Brooklyn. The *Washington Post* gave a detailed account of the sushi dinner that Linda Ragsdale, a children's-book illustrator from Nashville visiting India with a Virginia-based meditation group, was enjoying in the lobby café of the Oberoi hotel when she and her companions came under attack. One took in these humanizing details and immediately identified with the victims, vicariously feeling the horror they had suffered.[3]

The Mumbai terror lasted for almost three days. During the more than seven year long period prior to this ghastly event, the US-led invasions of Afghanistan and Iraq, Israel's targeted assassination of Palestinians (with large numbers of collateral victims in both Palestine and Lebanon), and the incarceration of 1.5 million Palestinians in Gaza (a place that humanitarian agencies have labelled "the largest prison on earth") had resulted in hundreds of thousands of deaths—655,000 in Iraq alone before 2006, according to conservative estimates of the Lancet Report—and millions of refugees.[4] Afghan and Iraqi civilians were constant casualties— at weddings and in schoolyards, hospital wards, and houses of worship. Afghan and Iraqi inmates have been tortured at Bagram Airbase, Abu Ghraib, and Guantanamo Bay. Abeer Qassim Hamza al-Janabi, a young Iraqi girl, was gang-raped by US marines, then murdered along with her parents and siblings, their bodies burnt. Among a number of massacres was the one in Hadithah, northwest of Baghdad. This was where US marines killed dozens of Iraqi civilians, including women and children, who were in their custody and entirely at their mercy.[5] The Quran has been flushed down the toilet and used for target practice in American torture chambers. In occupied Palestine, generations of Palestinians have fallen victim to the Israeli killing machine, their land stolen from under their feet, the men murdered, the women widowed, the children (like Muhammad Jamal al-Durrah) killed by Israeli sharpshooters, the parents starved by military blockade (aided and abetted by the United States and the European Union), while the world stood silently by and watched, evidently satisfied to pay the price of the Jewish Shoa with the Palestinian Nakba.

Anyone living in the United States during the past 30 years who has read the major newspapers, magazines and internet news, and watched news from the major radio and television networks, would be hard pressed to find anything resembling the justifiable outrage at the Mumbai mayhem in coverage of the infinitely more murderous acts of the United States and its allies in Afghanistan and Iraq or Israel in Palestine and Lebanon. What we do see is anger against the events of November 26–29, 2008, in Mumbai—or of September 11, 2001, in New York or March 11, 2004, in Madrid or July 7,

2005, in London—blown up into political outrage at Muslims in particular and Islam in general. The question is: Why?

Consider this contrast between Europe and North America: As the BBC was reporting the horrors of Mumbai in detail, its producers and reporters went out of their way to find young male British citizens of South Asian origin—the same age and ethnicity as the rampaging criminals—who were either lying wounded in Indian hospitals or landing at London's Heathrow airport to recount the horrors in accents familiar to the British audience; thus the criminal acts of a band of militant adventurers were kept from being generalized, politicized, and cited as an excuse for racists in Europe to use against immigrant communities. A similar scenario unfolded after the terrorist attacks of July 7, 2005, in London, when Mayor Ken Livingstone and other authorities and news organizations explicitly exonerated British Muslims and South Asian communities from any shred of complicity. In my more than 30 years in the United States, not once have I seen anything similar from an American news outlet. On the contrary. Mayor Rudolph Giuliani seemed to implicate Islam itself in the criminal events of September 11, 2001, thereby potentially putting millions of American Muslims at risk.

This assumption of collective Muslim guilt is a common staple of the American mass media. A particular paragon of twisted reasoning is the *New York Times* columnist Thomas Friedman, who wondered why Muslims around the globe (not just Pakistanis) did not "take to the streets to protest the mass murders of real people ... in Mumbai?"[6] Why would they do so when their Prophet is caricatured in Danish newspapers, he asked, but stay home when real human beings had been murdered? This was not irony or satire; the man was serious. But why should Muslims "take to the streets" to protest the Mumbai murders—what did they have to do with them?

Friedman's answer was:

> Because it takes a village. The best defense against this kind of murderous violence is to limit the pool of recruits, and the only way to do that is for the home society to isolate, condemn and denounce publicly and repeatedly the murderers—and not amplify, ignore, glorify, justify or explain their activities.[7]

Really? Can we reverse the angle? How many Americans were ready to "isolate, condemn and denounce publicly and repeatedly" the murders for which George W. Bush, Dick Cheney, and Donald

Rumsfeld were responsible—and how exactly do you "isolate" the elected officials of a democracy? No Muslims elected the mass murderers in Mumbai to any office. They were part of a criminal gang in whose creation US foreign policy, Saudi money, and Pakistani intelligence are all deeply implicated. But Bush and company were elected, and they are responsible for infinitely more murders in Iraq and Afghanistan. How many Jews worldwide "took to the streets" to protest the Zionist armed robbery of another people's homeland, or Baruch Goldstein's lethal rampage in Hebron against people praying in a mosque, or the starvation of 1.5 million human beings in Gaza, or the theft of Palestinian lands in broad daylight by murderous settlers who shoot to kill any Palestinian who dares to raise a voice, or the deliberate deaths of Palestinian children at the hands of Israeli army sharpshooters?[8] Did Christians around the globe "take to the streets" in 1995, when Timothy McVeigh blew up a federal building in Oklahoma, killing 168 people? Did they "take to the streets" in 2007, when mass murderer Seung-Hui Cho murdered 33 students on the campus of Virginia Tech—one for every year of Jesus Christ's life? Or, did they "take to the streets" between 1972 and 1976, when another Christian serial killer, John Wayne Gacy, raped and murdered 33 boys and young men—also one for every year of Christ's life? Did Hindus around the globe "take to the streets" in 2002, when Hindu mobs raped Muslim women in public, tore their pregnant bellies open and skewered their unborn children? Then why expect Muslims to act differently to other people? The last time millions upon millions of human beings—including Muslims, Jews, Christians, Hindus, agnostics, and atheists—poured into the streets worldwide was on February 15, 2003, against the atrocities of the American government in Afghanistan which, supported by Friedman and his employers at the *New York Times*, it was about to repeat in Iraq.

Friedman's demand was, of course, entirely rhetorical. Yet it defies reason that he could, with a single column, criminalize the more than 1.5 billion Muslims—a quarter of the world's population. How could this be the common wisdom of a nation, a people, a country—an empire?

What one could criticize in the United States in the aftermath of the events of 9/11 were the activities of the American news media—and in particular "the Newspaper of Record", The *New York Times*—in beating the drums of war, initially against Afghanistan and soon after against Iraq. A case in point is that of *New York Times* reporter Judith Miller, who failed to properly question or verify what she was told by Iraqi exiles and US officials while an embedded reporter in Iraq prior to the invasion.[9] Indeed, in the crescendo of events building up to both wars, one could have been excused if one had believed that the *New York Times* was, in effect, the official mouthpiece of the Bush administration.[10]

In place of critical journalism attempting to inform or soul-search, the American public got attacks on Muslims by such dyed-in-the-wool Islamophobes as Daniel Pipes and David Horowitz—and by far more reputable scholars. The Harvard legal scholar Alan Dershowitz argued for the legalization of torture of "suspected terrorists" just before revelations emerged of US torture chambers at Abu Ghraib Prison and elsewhere.[11] Like Dershowitz, who made his case from within the bosom of Western jurisprudence, the human-rights scholar Michael Ignatieff has made his own arguments from within the Western human-rights discourse.[12] And then there was Obsession, an Islamophobic documentary produced by the Canadian-Israeli rabbi Raphael Shore, which aimed to influence American voters against Barack Obama and in favor of John McCain.[13] In George W. Bush's America (up to and including the presidential election of 2008), it was open season on Islam.

What could account for this discrepancy—outrage at criminal acts when the perpetrators are Muslims, yet complacency toward far worse acts when they are aimed against Muslims? How would one understand this systematic dehumanization of Arabs and Muslims— as beings capable only of criminal acts (when a mere handful have perpetrated them) coupled with disregard for their sufferings when millions of them are victims? I remember seeing Harold Bloom's learned volume *Shakespeare: The Invention of the Human* in a New York bookstore in 1999 and wondering about those who have not or cannot read Shakespeare—are they not human? If you prick them, will they not bleed? I had the same reaction to Steven Spielberg's 2005 film Munich. Every time we see the Israelis plotting to murder a Palestinian in revenge for the 1972 Munich Olympic attack they are eating and drinking; yet never do we see their Palestinian targets so much as sipping a glass of water. Why? Do Palestinians not eat—if you prick them, will they not scream? Why the humanizing effects for the Israeli assassins but never for their Palestinian victims—who, it turns out, actually had nothing to do with the Munich attack?

The problem is how to account for this endemic and enduring dehumanization? Whence its origin, wherefore its functions? We might explain away the paltriness of outrage in the North American and Western European press over Afghan, Iraqi, or Palestinians victims of imperial arrogance by pointing out the hypocrisy of double standards. But that explanation suggests a fundamental indecency in human beings which it seems only proper to reject as demeaning and fallacious. The compelling question remains: Why is it that death and destruction causes so much loathing and outrage when it takes place in Mumbai, London, Tel Aviv, or New York and not when it is multiplied ten thousandfold in Baghdad, Kandahar, Beirut, or Gaza City? The answer cannot be sought in the sandy domains of malice and malevolence. It must be carefully cultivated in the immediate historical vicinities where the politics of despair and the economics of domination combine to create a moral mandate to divide and rule—where some are perceived as more human than others.

THE IDEOLOGICAL SOCIETY

My principal argument in this book is that in present-day North America and Western Europe—and by extension the world they seek to dominate—brown has become the new black and Muslims the new Jews. This is because a recodification of racist power relations is the modus operandi of an ever-changing condition of domination in which capital continually creates its own elusive cultures. My concern, as a result, is with the manner in which ideologies are formed at the heart of the entity that comprises the American empire and its allies. My goal is to foreground an ongoing discrepancy between fact and fantasy that dehistoricizes the criminal events of September 11, 2001, in the US, or July 7, 2005, in London, or March 11, 2004, in Madrid, or November 26–29, 2008, in Mumbai, into political events (with blatant racist implications against Islam in general and Muslims in particular), while at the same time sanitizing the United States' imperialist adventurism (most recently in Afghanistan and Iraq) and the armed robbery of the Palestinians' homeland by a band of European colonialists that calls itself Israel—a process by which the Western imperialist powers have come to appear as legitimate and even innocent bystanders, and even, victims of a global barbarism targeting their Western civilization. This inversion of facts by fantasy, of truth by politics is of central importance to my argument. My purpose is to develop a critical inroad, which I will call "native informer", into the workings of an ideological society perhaps unprecedented in history.

Predicated on what William Kornhauser identified in 1959 as mass society,[14] wherein individuals are seen as atomized into defenseless entities outside any institutional support against fascist, totalitarian, and (one might add) self-delusional tendencies, and on what Guy Debord termed in 1967 the society of the spectacle (*la société du spectacle*),[15] wherein the lived experiences of such atomized individuals are ontologically replaced with their representations, the ideological society designates America and her allies' systematic consensus building for military adventurism around the globe on the threshold of the twenty-first century. A combination of historical events, sociological developments, metaphysical convictions, and fetishized visual representations have ripened conditions for the production of an indoctrinated and gullible mass—a society held together neither by a single religion nor by any other shared conception of sanctity, nor even by a common bourgeois morality. An abiding conviction as to its own historical singularity holds the ideological society together.

Kornhauser and Debord drew on ideas by Erich Fromm (*The Fear of Freedom*, 1942) and David Riesman (*The Lonely Crowd*, 1950), theorists chiefly concerned with the rise of fascism, as well as on Marx's notion of alienation and Durkheim's concept of anomie. These were the conceptual forerunners of the "ideological society" that I propose here, held together neither by the institutions of civil society nor by the populist apparatus of a fascist party but rather by unexamined (and unexaminable) ideological convictions and assumptions. The ideological society is thus predicated on what Robert Bellah has called a "civil religion"—an amorphous proposition always at the mercy of capital's vicissitudes.[16]

Much earlier, Alexis de Tocqueville (1805–59) recognized the fascistic, censorial forces that hid within the democratic proclivities of the United States and gave rise to its ideological homogeneity. He wrote in his revelatory Democracy in America:

I know no country in which, speaking generally, there is less independence of mind and true freedom of discussion than in America. In America, the majority has enclosed thought within a formidable fence. A writer is free inside that area, but woe to the man who goes beyond it.[17]

More than a century before Foucault's *Discipline and Punish* (1975), Tocqueville noted that:

formerly tyranny used the clumsy weapons of chains and hangmen; nowadays even despotism, though it seemed to have nothing more to learn, has been perfected by civilization. Princes made violence a physical thing, but our contemporary democratic republics have turned it into something as intellectual as the human will is intended to constrain. Under the absolute government of a single man, despotism, to reach the soul, clumsily struck at the body, and the soul, escaping from such blows, rose gloriously above it; but in democratic republics that is not at all how tyranny behaves; it leaves the body alone and goes straight to the soul.

His conclusion was:

In the proudest nations of the Old World works were published which faithfully portrayed the vices and absurdities of contem- poraries...But the power that dominates in the United States does not understand being mocked like that. The least reproach offends it, and the slightest sting of truth turns it fierce, and one must praise everything, from the turn of its phrases to its most robust virtues. No writer, no matter how famous, can escape from this obligation to sprinkle incense over his fellow citizens. Hence the majority lives in a state of perpetual self-adoration; only strangers or experience may be able to bring certain truth to the Americans' attention.[18]

"The power that dominates in the United States" still works the same way, unwilling to tolerate the slightest suggestion of culpability for the crimes that it has perpetrated around the globe. At the heart of the ideological society lies the conviction of a moral mission, even a divine destiny, authorizing its almost inadvertent drive towards global domination.

That there is something profoundly Christian about this metaphysical assumption is evident in the missionary zeal with which Americans go about seeking to control the world and save it from itself. That the world does not fully appreciate this intervention on its behalf seems seriously to baffle Americans. The result is more than a mere will to dominate, or to assert the superiority of the imperial culture over the varied cultures of the natives—from native Americans to native Iraqis. There is even a note of tragic melancholy in American imperialism, perhaps best represented by Ethan Edwards, the character John Wayne plays in John Ford's 1956 film *The Searchers*, and captured in the very last shot of the film: Ethan brings his niece Debbie (Natalie Wood) back from native American captivity and she and the family all go inside as Ethan stands alone. After a short pause, Ethan turns and walks back towards the empty desert.[19]

Something in American imperialism needs to rescue a world it sees as caught in native barbarity, to make it safe for mortal humanity and the immortal idea of "America". All American superheroes from Spiderman to Batman are invariably lonely creatures aware that "with great power comes great responsibility"—which precludes their marrying and having families. American imperialism is not about denying the natives their history and culture; it is just better that these backward cultures (and by that they mean no disrespect) see the light of day and do as Americans do—except that Americans themselves have come to no consensus as to what it is that they do. A Wall Street meltdown sends everyone running for the basest common ideology: survival of the fittest. I would even shrink from calling to mind the notion that at the bottom of American imperialism is "racism" (despite the abundance of racism in America)—for it is not as Caucasians or Christians that they seek to save the world. It is as "Americans"—that most amorphous of concepts. Something about being American demands saving the world even if that means destroying it.

AN EMPIRE WITH OR WITHOUT HEGEMONY: THE MAKING OF ISLAMOPHOBIA

Capital is ideologically promiscuous—prepared to dominate any culture. If blacks (as African slaves) and Jews (as European immigrants) were the white supremacists' nightmare of yesteryear, capital can posit the brown and the Muslim as the contemporary "other" and proceed with its business of dividing and ruling. The key question is the manner in which American imperialism works—with or without hegemony.

The nature of American empire has been the subject of many fine studies. V. G. Kiernan's America: *The New Imperialism: From White Settlement to World Hegemony* (1978/2005) still stands as a solid historical account of the imperialist drive. More recent work, in the aftermath of the invasions of Afghanistan and Iraq, ranges from Walter Nugent's *Habits of Empire* (2008), which argues that the United States has had imperial proclivities from its very inception, to Chalmers Johnson's *Blowback Trilogy* (2000–08), which examines the political and moral consequences of today's globalized American Empire.[20]

Since the late 1980s, however, these inquiries have been cast in civilizational terms, most famously by two American political strategists: Francis Fukuyama in his 1989 essay "The End of History?", later expanded into *The End of History and the Last Man*, and Samuel Huntington in his 1993 essay "Clash of Civilizations", later expanded into *The Clash of Civilizations and the Remaking of World Order*. Though their conclusions are popularly cast as contradictory, with Huntington answering Fukuyama, they are in fact complementary. Fukuyama declares that Western liberal democracy has triumphed over all the alternatives; Huntington recasts this triumphalist idea in the language of conflict, proposing that Western civilization now faces great threats from its Islamic and Chinese nemeses. While Fukuyama's 1989 essay coincides with— and celebrates—the demise of the Soviet Union and the Eastern bloc and the rise of a unipolar US imperialism, Huntington's 1993 essay coincides with the first attempt to bring down the World Trade Center, on February 26, 1993, by a band of militant Muslims. Thus, between the collapse of the Berlin Wall and the first attack on the World Trade Center—namely, the period of George H. W. Bush's presidency and the rise of what he termed the "New World Order"—Soviet communism yielded to Islamism as the West's new nemesis. The two essays dovetail beautifully. For about four years, the West was in a state of limbo, not quite knowing what to do with itself after Fukuyama (remembering his Hegel and forgetting his Karl Schmitt) declared it triumphant, until Huntington (forgetting his Hegel and remembering his Karl Schmitt) manufactured a new global enemy for it.

Although Fukuyama's and Huntington's theses have been discussed primarily in the light of their foreign-policy implications, a major target of this rise in civilizational thinking, as I have argued elsewhere in detail, was demographic changes within the United States.[21] Soon after the Immigration and Nationality Act Amendment of 1965 (the Hart-Cellar Act) abolished national origin quotas, a noticeable rise in immigration resulted in major demographic changes. During the 1970s, for every seven Latin-American and Asian immigrants only one Western European came to the United States; during the 1980s, for every six Latin American and Asian immigrants, only one Western European came.[22] The sudden interest in defending or eulogizing Western civilization by such scholars as Alan Bloom (*The Closing of the American Mind*,

1987) and Jacques Barzun (*From Dawn to Decadence: 500 Years of Western Cultural Life, 1500 to the Present, 2000*) was a direct response to these demographic changes. The shift was particularly evident on the university campuses where these new immigrants came to study; hence the wars over the core curriculum, with one side defending the study of Western literature, art, music, sciences, and the other arguing for a more global approach, often coalesced around demands for race and ethnic studies.[23]

While both neoconservative ideology and civilizational thinking are of European origin, they came to American shores via Leo Strauss and his students and disciples at the University of Chicago, who included both Bloom and Fukuyama.[24] The link between Strauss and the Nazi political theorist Karl Schmitt is of paramount importance here[25]—for it is Schmitt's concept of "the enemy"[26] that through Strauss, then Fukuyama and Huntington, gradually narrows in on Islam. The most important regional factors contributing to the perception of Islam and Islamism as the bête noire of the West were the 1977–79 Islamic revolution in Iran, the formation of Hezbollah in the aftermath of the 1982 Israeli invasion of Lebanon, the emergence of Hamas in Palestine after the commencement of the First Intifada in 1987, and the emergence of Groupe Islamique Armé in Algeria after the country's military government annulled the victory of the Islamic Salvation Front in the 1992 general elections.

The emergence of Islam as the nemesis of the West gave a new lease of life to old-fashioned Orientalism. Among those who have made careers out of glorifying Western civilization and lamenting its vulnerability to the threat of Islam, no one could outdo Bernard Lewis, professor emeritus of Near Eastern studies at Princeton, who began his career in the intelligence corps of the British army and ended it as a consultant to the Pentagon—thus linking British colonialism and American imperialism in the span of a single life. In half a century of writings, Lewis has systematically depicted Islam as a fundamental threat to the uniquely lofty ideals of the West. As early as the 1950s he had envisioned the clash of civilizations, and to this day he remains incensed that the idea is credited to Samuel Huntington. Since the early 1960s, he has published books which repeatedly rattle on about the innate opposition of the two sides, including *The Middle East and the West* (1964), *Islam and the West* (1994), *Cultures in Conflict* (1996), *The Muslim Discovery of Europe* (2001), and *What Went Wrong* (2003), laying the groundwork for Fukuyama and Huntington.

The political factor that globalized the popularity of grand strategists like Fukuyama and Huntington was the emergence of a unipolar international system dominated by the United States and its allies following the collapse of the Soviet Union—a new situation that soon gave rise to neoconservatism in political ideology and neoliberalism in global economics. The Project for the New American Century (PNAC), an organization founded in 1997 by William Kristol and Robert Kagan, became the intellectual powerhouse supporting American military supremacy. (Among its members were not only Fukuyama but also Donald Rumsfeld and Paul Wolfowitz, who would serve as Secretary and Deputy Secretary of Defense under George W. Bush.) By January 1998, PNAC was so assured in its mission that it was encouraging President Clinton to remove Saddam Hussein from power. By 2000, the ideas of Fukuyama and Huntington had so utterly stormed Washington that militant Islamism had moved to the center of its short attention span—entirely shorn, of course, of the Reaganite context in which the United States had been an active agent in its rise via enthusiastic support for the anti-Soviet mujahedeen in Afghanistan.

THE NATIVE INFORMER

Let us consider the case of Azar Nafisi and her book *Reading Lolita in Tehran* (2003), a titillating tale of a Persian harem with the women waiting for the US marines to rescue them from their own menfolk.[27] The conceptual category that best comprehends the services that Nafisi and others like her have provided the US imperial project under George W. Bush's administration is the notion of the "native informer", a potent component of neoconservative ideology that I plan to develop and expose in some detail in this book.

The term native informant (as opposed to native informer) was first used by Adam Shatz in reference to Fouad Ajami.[28] In honor of John Ford's 1935 masterpiece *The Informer*—with its archetypal squealer, Gypo Nolan (Victor McLaglen), betraying the Irish Republican Army militant Frankie McPhillip (Wallace Ford)—I have modified informant to informer. Where informant credits comprador intellectuals with the knowledge they claim to possess but in fact do not, informer suggests the moral degeneration specific to the act of betrayal. The record of Fouad Ajami and Kanan Makiya, two prominent native informers who predicted that in response to the US invasion the Iraqis would pour into their streets bearing flowers and sweets, is a case in point. These informers are more effective in manufacturing the public illusions that empires need to sustain themselves than in truly informing the public about the cultures they denigrate and dismiss.

Gayatri Spivak has written of the native informant as "a certain postcolonial subject" who has "been recoding the colonial subject and appropriating the native informant's position. Today, with globalization in full swing, telecommunicative informatics taps the native informant directly in the name of indigenous knowledge and advances biopiracy."[29] Spivak identifies the native informant as what "encrypts the name of man". In "Writing Culture: Postmodernism and Ethnography", Mahmut Mutman moves forward to the even more daring proposition that the foreclosure that the native informant posits, in Spivak's terms, is in fact "the Western man's erasure of his own origin".[30] These critiques of anthropological ethnography and the role of the native informant within it (a direction I am not going to pursue in this book), which take the entire discipline of anthropology to task, descend from Talal Asad's pioneering essay in his 1973 *Anthropology and the Colonial Encounter* and from Edward Said's 1989 "Representing the Colonized: Anthropology's Interlocutors" and appear most recently in the work of George Marcus and Nicholas De Genova.[31] According to this line of argument, the term native informant is particularly applicable to contemporary anthropologists of Arab and Muslim origins, trained in European and American universities in the deep colonial grammar of their discipline, who turn the members of their own families and the fate of their own native countries into objects of anthropological curiosity. Generations of them have been exposed to Asad's groundbreaking assertion that the discipline must move "from the history of colonial anthropology to the anthropology of western hegemony", yet they continue to do the "field work" of European and American anthropologists in their own homeland.[32]

My own primary concern is with native informers who have emigrated and serve the empire on its home front. They have provided a crucial service without which the theses of grand strategists like Fukuyama and Huntington would have been relegated to administrative or academic circles without much effect on shaping opinions, building consensus, and facilitating war. By proposing Nafisi's *Reading Lolita in Tehran* as the necessary emotive addendum to Fukuyama and Huntington/Lewis's dual thesis of civilizational conflict, I wish to investigate the way grand strategies of domination become operational through the compradorial function of the native informers.

The publication of *Reading Lolita in Tehran*, to which I devote a chapter, capped the long rise of neoconservatism: the collapse of the Soviet Union (1989), the emergence of the unipolar international system dominated by the United States (1980–88), Fukuyama's triumphalist postulation of the US as the normative culmination of the Hegelian Geist (1989), and Huntington's constitution of Islam as the arch-nemesis of the West (1993), all predicated on Lewis's lifelong dedication to the same proposition. Nafisi emigrated from her native Iran after a short academic career, becoming a protégé of Lewis's, a colleague of Ajami's, and an employee of Paul Wolfowitz's (who would serve as Deputy Secretary of Defense under Donald Rumsfeld) at Johns Hopkins's Paul H. Nitze School of Advanced International Studies. She published her memoir at a time when 9/11 had traumatized the American public and given its neoconservative leaders an excuse to launch their carefully planned "Project for a New American Century".

The history of US-Iranian hostility began with the CIA-engineered coup of 1953. More than 25 years of subsequent US military support for the dictatorial monarchy of Mohammad Reza Shah Pahlavi generated resentment in a wide cross-section of Iranian society, climaxing with the Islamic Revolution and the formation of an Islamic Republic that became a thorn in the side of American and Israeli militarism, with the potential for spreading its ideology like wildfire. During the Reagan administration (1981–89), the United States and its European and regional allies (Saudi Arabia, Pakistan, and Israel in particular) created bumper zones on either side of the Islamic Republic, overseen by the Wahabi-inspired Taliban to its east and Saddam Hussein to its west. The Taliban succeeded in expelling the Soviets from Afghanistan and in preventing the spread of the Shi'i-inspired Iranian revolution to Central Asia. Saddam Hussein did the same (likewise heavily supported by the US and its allies) by engaging Iran in a war that lasted eight terrible years (1980–88), with Muslims murdering Muslims by the tens of thousands, much to the satisfaction of such observers as former Secretary of State Henry Kissinger, who quipped, "It's a pity both sides can't lose". The two Frankensteins the US created—Mullah Omar in Afghanistan and Saddam Hussein in Iraq—succeeded at their assigned tasks, but they came back to haunt their creators. Saddam Hussein had scarcely finished battling Iran when he turned the same weapons and intelligence that the US and its allies had put at his disposal on Kuwait; the Taliban that the Reagan administration had trained (through Pakistan) and financed (through Saudi Arabia) became the host of Osama bin Laden and al-Qaeda, whose wave of reported terrorist attacks (there is no way to verify the charges) against the United States and its interests ranged from Nairobi, Kenya (1998) and Dar as-Salam, Tanzania (1998), to the World Trade Center (1993 and 2001). Thus *Reading Lolita in Tehran* became a bestseller in Bush's America at a time when the Soviet Union had fallen, US-supported Islamism had turned against its benefactors, the Islamic Republic of Iran was becoming belligerent, and Hamas and Hezbollah had grown politically potent in Lebanon and Palestine.

In my chapter on *Reading Lolita in Tehran*, I offer up Nafisi as the character type—the theoretical template—of the native informer, which has served as a major device for legitimizing neoconservative ideology in the American empire, corroborating Fukuyama's and Huntington's dual theses. Rooted in the post-1965 changes to immigration law, it is a direct result of intellectual migration, the so-called brain drain: comprador intellectuals came to the United States in search of fame and fortune. As such it calls for a careful conceptualization and typification in the classical Weberian sense of an "Ideal-Type", or a unit of sociological analysis in the tradition of his "interpretative sociology" (verstehende Soziologie).

The typical native informers, born and raised in places such as Iran, Lebanon, Somalia, and Pakistan, move to Europe and/or the United States for their higher education. They may come from modest or opulent backgrounds; their financial means may be either inherited, the result of advantageous marriage, or payment for services to their American employers. They rarely hold a stable job with professional accountability, remaining rather on the professional margins of the society whose interests they serve. Whether or not they have made a career in their native land, they have always felt alienated from it, but they are no more at home in the country they have adopted just because it is where they can sell their services best. Their image of the adopted country, however, is very much white-identified; they are thus angry and baffled to find many other brown immigrants like themselves, rude compatriots who watch them closely and occasionally even have the audacity to expose them.

This character type has been pinpointed before, notably in Harriet Beecher Stowe's Uncle Tom and Malcolm X's House Negro. There is, of course, a fundamental difference between the contemporary version, who is more brownish than black, and their antecedents from the nineteenth and twentieth centuries. Uncle Tom has evolved into Auntie Azar and Uncle Fouad, well-educated and sophisticated enough to disguise their obsequiousness toward their white employers and audiences.

Most important, they can feign authority while telling their conquerors not what they need to know but what they want to hear. (In return, American and European liberals call them "voices of dissent".) Faced with the Islamophobic conditions of their new homes, they have learned the art of simultaneously acknowledging and denying their Muslim origins. They speak English with an accent that confirms their authenticity to their white interlocutors. The recent incidents of urban terrorism have been so good for their business that they have had to hire PR firms (such as Benador Associates)[33] to negotiate their speaking fees and manage their media appearances.

In his groundbreaking study. *War on Terror, Inc: Corporate Profiteering from the Politics of Fear* (2007), Solomon Hughes has documented the massive industry that benefits from fear-mongering and the depiction of Muslims as the enemy of the West. He devotes a chapter to the lucrative propaganda front from which enterprising native informers have much benefited. It does not, however, fully attend to the wave of fake memoirs that flooded the market at the same time as *Reading Lolita in Tehran*. Perhaps the most notorious example was Norma Khouri's bestselling *Forbidden Love* (2003), a fabricated account of a supposed friend's honor killing perpetrated after she was discovered to have had a love affair (with "a Christian army officer", no less). Malcolm Knox of the *Sydney Morning Herald* exposed Khouri as a fraud, forcing her publisher, Random House, to recall the book in some markets.[34]

Natives informing on their brothers and sisters back in the field as a way of ingratiating themselves with their white masters have been a major character type since at least the time of Harriet Beecher Stowe, a pathology created by the condition of coloniality. In George W. Bush's America the practice was perfected to ever more lucrative levels, with a publishing ear perfectly pitched to what would sell in a society deeply traumatized by seeing two of its tallest landmarks cut down in broad daylight.

This market, which flourished at the cost of demonizing 1.5 billion human beings, was on the lookout for the best and the brightest—individuals with a pigment to their complexion who could tell their tales with an accent to their English. The native informers stepped forward to oblige, accommodate, and entertain as the US military machinery flexed its muscles around the Muslim world. Many of them were adopted by the US military (Seyyed

Vali Reza Nasr and Ray Takeyh), or by key figures in the military establishment (Azar Nafisi and Fouad Ajami), or by neoconservative think-tanks (Ayaan Hirsi Ali), or in a few cases by no one in particular (Salman Rushdie and Ibn Warraq) because they provided a cover of legitimacy to American imperial designs on the Islamic world. They have undertaken their activities in the honorable name of defending the human rights, women's rights, and civil rights of Muslims themselves—and the relative lack of those rights in Muslim countries gave them the space and legitimacy they required. The blatant manner in which these native informers have demonized their own cultures and societies is made possible by the protection they enjoy when they relocate to the centers of Western European and North American power. For obvious reasons it would have been much too risky to produce such serviceable knowledge from Tehran, Baghdad, Beirut, Karachi, or Mogadishu. The phenomena of globalization in general and labor migration in particular have combined to create the conditio sine qua non for these comprador intellectuals.

All the native informers I discuss in this book are of Muslim origin. They have all also consistently denigrated Islam, in both its cultural and religious aspects. While the context in the United States is American imperialism, in Europe it is racist indignation and legalized prejudice against Muslim immigrant communities—South Asians in the United Kingdom, North Africans in France, Turks in Germany, Iraqis and Palestinians in the Scandinavian countries. The rise of the fascist right in Eastern and Northern Europe has given ample space for native informers like Ayaan Hirsi Ali to supply ammunition to the racism already evident in the statements of the late Italian journalist Oriana Fallaci and the French cinema icon Brigitte Bardot. Italian Prime Minister Silvio Berlusconi has also been loose with his language and Pope Benedict XVI has made overtly anti-Islamic statements. Their statements have also been bolstered by native informers. Indeed, such individuals bearing terrible tales about Islam are particularly popular with Christian fundamentalists and zealous Zionists in both the United States and Europe.

Native informers like Hirsi Ali, Nafisi, and Irshad Manji are paraded before their North American and Western European audiences as "voices of dissent" against the innate and enduring barbarity of Islam. The pathology they nurture grows with every atrocity by or against Muslims, and it is bound to continue to be exacerbated as the US/Israeli war against Muslims deepens. The

Americans turn to expatriate intellectuals to tell populations targeted for liberation (Afghans, Iraqis, Somalis, Palestinians, Iranians) that they intend to invade, bomb, and occupy their homelands for those populations' own good. But the primary target of this propaganda is first and foremost the Americans themselves, who need to be assured that they are a good, noble, and superior people, ordained by their creator to rescue the world from its evils. The messages the native informers carry include "Just look at the condition of women in the Islamic Republic!" (or Afghanistan, or Iraq), "They can't even read a masterpiece of Western literature like Lolita in peace!" and "We have to liberate these young women from their bondage!" Western civilization (the code term of this ideology), Western literature, even the English language become the vehicle of this humanitarian mission to rescue Muslim women. Rushdie, Nafisi, Warraq, Manji, Hirsi Ali, and Ajami all serve to remind Americans and convince non-Americans alike of the sublimity of Western literature, art, and music.

What we are witnessing, as a result, is a whole new mode of knowledge production about the Orient (basically, the entire world beyond Western Europe and North America)—a form of knowledge produced under duress. In classical European Orientalism, a whole language, discourse, and ideology were crafted by the imperialists themselves to maintain their domination as natural and inevitable.[35] The native informers have digested and internalized this language and now speak it with the authority of natives. There is no longer any need for "expert knowledge" when you can hear the facts from the horse's mouth.

By "native informers" I do not refer to those translators in Iraq, Afghanistan, or Palestine—collaborators paid for their incorporation into the massive military-intelligence machinery that facilitates the daily operation of the occupation. I even exempt those professors of Arabic or Persian who are offered inviting salaries (plus green cards for the entire family, in one case I know of) for leaving their university posts to teach these "security languages" (as Arabic, Persian, and Urdu are called) in military academies. But I do include such people as Seyyed Vali Reza Nasr and Abbas Milani, who use the muddy waters of war to advance their careers by abandoning academic life to join military and/or intelligence outlets, or to become spin doctors on current affairs. These kind of activities, in effect, all serve to rationalize and justify US carnage in the Muslim world.

"A democratic public", Tocqueville once said of America, "often treats its authors much as kings usually behave towards their courtiers: it enriches and despises them. What more do the venal souls who are born in courts or deserve to live there merit?"[36]

AFTER FANON AND ON THE OTHER SIDE OF SAID

Whence this playing politics with the truth, this inversion of fact by fantasy, whereby the victims become victimizers, the terrorized terrorists, whereby those targeted by the Israeli sharpshooters and Zionist colonial settlers become the criminals and their tormentors the victims? The native informer plays a key role in making the inversion of fact by fantasy appear logical. But where did these native informers come from? What is their genealogy, their pathology, their point of origin (and return)?

In his pioneering 1952 study of the relationship between racism and colonialism, *Black Skin, White Masks* (*Peau noire, masques blancs*), Frantz Fanon relied heavily on psychoanalytic theory to understand the traumatic sense of inferiority that overtakes those who fall prey to the racist assumptions of the supremacist forces dominating their homelands. Fanon conducted his study during the French occupation of Algeria, in the twilight of European colonialism; his principal objective was to see through the desubjection that colonized people experienced—the process by which normatively divided, self-alienated black subjects internalized their anger and redirected it against themselves. The colonial apparatus, Fanon believed, successfully manufactures a profound sense of inferiority in the colonized subjects that leads them—actively or passively, consciously or subconsciously—to identify with and seek to serve the colonial agency. The bourgeoisie and upwardly mobile comprador intellectuals, he argued, are particularly susceptible.

In *Black Skin, White Masks*, Fanon psychoanalyzed the early pathology of what would grow into today's native informer. The white masks Fanon identified, however, were donned on the colonial ground, while the masks I identify in this study have made the journey abroad. They are like Mustafa Sa'eed in Tayeb Salih's 1966 novel *Season of Migration to the North*, who does not return to Sudan when Great Britain invades Sudan but rather stays in England, looking for a good job and using his knowledge of Arabic and of Africa to tell the British what they want to hear. Fanon's themes reverberate in Aimé Césaire's *A Discourse on Colonialism* (1953), Albert Memmi's *The Colonizer and the Colonized* (1957), Ashis

Nandy's *Intimate Enemies* (1983), all the way down to Edward Said's *Culture and Imperialism* (1994). In all these pioneering cases, we see the colonized subjugated to their colonizers' assumption of cultural superiority. Shakespeare becomes beautiful because the sun never sets on the British Empire—and Kiarostami becomes a great filmmaker only after the French celebrate him at Cannes.

The principal function of these theories—from Fanon to Said and on to Césaire, Memmi, and Nandy—has been to liberate the colonized mind from the trap of that slavish identification with power. One sees much of that slavish disposition in the native informer, but on the imperial home front, where consensus is being manufactured, that psychopathology has now transformed into career opportunism. Native informers have immersed themselves in the white-identified culture and they now serve it out of pure careerism. Good native informers are paid well.

My intention is to extend Fanon's insights into the contemporary context of the American "War on Terror" via Said's notion of "intellectual exile", in order to show the darker side of intellectual migration. While Said celebrated the positive aspects of intellectuals in exile, at odds with the power of states—and while I recognize the emancipatory force of that exile insofar as Said himself personified it—I wish to map out the conditions in which from the selfsame cadre of exiles are recruited native informers who are no longer telling their imperial employers what they need to know but rather what they want to believe in order to manufacture communal consensus. They are there to convince the public that invading and bombing and occupying the homelands of others is a good and moral thing. I write toward an understanding of the ideological machinations of imperial domination in a new world beyond national polities, economies, and cultures, sustained via disposable forms of knowledge produced by immigrant intellectuals. Homeless compradors can become mercenary minds: native informers with no loyalty to any particular nation or commitment to any particular cause.

BROWN IS THE NEW BLACK

In what follows, I pursue an argument about the conditions under which the figure of the native informer has assumed a key function in the American ideological machinery. In making this machinery, I wish to argue, brown has become the new black and the Muslim has emerged as the new Jew. White stays the same, but it has lost its iconic power to name, color, and designate. It is imperative at the outset not to essentialize or fetishize any of these colors: capital is promiscuous, married to no particular culture of domination. Black-and-white was yesterday, brown-and-white is today, and tomorrow the color-coding apparatus of domination might yet again change. The Jew has served as the Christian's "other" for centuries, but now even Pope Benedict XVI has dug out medieval evidence that Muhammad was a false prophet. All prophets are false prophets in the logic of capital, until they prove handy to Nike in selling more of the shoes produced in sweatshops around the globe.

In constructing the prototype of the native informer in the following chapters, my only reason for having used some examples rather than others is that in the aftermath of the US-led invasions of Afghanistan and Iraq these figures emerged as the most publicly prominent voices among them. One might add quite a number of other figures to those I have examined in detail; Ayaan Hirsi Ali, Irshad Manji, Fouad Ajami, Salman Rushdie, and Kanan Makiya certainly deserve much more than the passing references I offer. But just about everything one might say about them is already present in what I say about the figures I do examine. To exhaust the supply would be impossible anyway, since they are increasing in number by the day (some of very low intellectual caliber, others with advanced degrees from great universities). These native informers are part of a much larger group of natives now serving the interests of America and its allies in various capacities—as translators and analysts in the military and the CIA, or FBI informers on Muslims in their communities, or members of think-tanks advising the US government. My intention, however, is to pinpoint the intellectual elite—the most publicly vocal, whose books and articles, TV, radio and internet appearances have been instrumental in manufacturing consent for the "war on terror"—which translates as old-fashioned imperialism with a moral vengeance. These native informers are vital in making the case for that moral vengeance in terms of human rights and especially women's rights.

The first chapter, "Brown Skin, White Masks", makes the case for the recodification of North American and Western European racism. I follow the logic of Fanon's argument to unearth the pathological origins of our contemporary native informers. The second chapter, "On Comprador Intellectuals", takes off from Said's notion of the exilic intellectual to show the darker side of that designation as the fertile ground for the breeding of native informers. In the third chapter, "Literature and Empire" (an earlier version of which was published in June 2006 in *Al-Ahram Weekly*), I turn my attention to Azar Nafisi in order to examine the renewed role of colonially-slanted "Western literature"[37] in promoting the cause of US imperialism. My objective is to demonstrate how with one strike Nafisi has provided this cause with three services, on both the home and battle fronts: (1) denigrating an entire culture of revolutionary resistance to colonialism; (2) advancing the cultural foregrounding of US imperialism; and (3) catering to recalcitrant forces within the United States who are waging war against immigrant communities seeking curricular recognition in the humanities and social sciences. These multiple tasks are the sort of services that make a native informer and a comprador intellectual exceedingly useful to the smooth operation of what aspires to be a global empire. The fourth chapter, "The House Muslim", concentrates on the case of the anonymous person who, under the pen name Ibn Warraq, has engaged in an extensive, systematic, well-funded and well-publicized vilification of Islam and Muslims. Ibn Warraq himself (or herself) does not really merit all that much attention, but by exposing the faulty bases of his (or her) writing I wish to show the deep desperation of this attempt to manufacture consent about the threat of Islam.

BEYOND FANON, AFTER SAID

My objective in examining native informers of different varieties is to mark a moment in the making and breaking of the globalized empire in which I live, and whose claim to moral authority must remain the subject of our sustained critical scrutiny. To do so, I remove the compradorial character of the native informer from its colonial confines and apply it to those intellectuals whom Said called "Aye-sayers" at the heart of the empire, the new vintage having migrated to the centers of power. Their principal function is less to decode their own culture for the conquerors than to manufacture justifications in a manner subservient to the conquerors' will to dominate. The most significant difference between Fanon and Said's understanding of the term and my own is that I have moved my theoretical frame of reference from the colonies to the heart of the empire. The work of these native informers—for example, Rushdie's and Warraq's essays, Hirsi Ali's and Nafisi's memoirs—is principally for American and European readers, and thus it is written in English (Their Arabic and/or Persian translations become quite curious oddities). For this reason, I make a specific distinction between the figure of the native informer and that of the collaborator. The latter tells the conquering power what it needs to know in order to better dominate, while the former tells it what it wants to hear in order to better sell its wars, particularly to its domestic audience. The collaborator provides factual and strategic knowledge, the native informer provides emotive vistas and ideological slants with which to criminalize any mode of resistance to domination. Ephialtes of Trachis, the grotesquely degenerate Greek who reportedly helped the Persian army in the battle of Thermopylae, is the model of the collaborator: he showed the Persians a hidden road to the back of the Spartan army. Ajami and Nafisi, in contrast, are not of value on the actual battlefield. They are useful to the empire within the suburban, SUV-swollen comfort of the imperial home front in Fairfax and Chevy Chase, where they support the belligerent powers through the liberating languages of human rights and women's rights.

My objective is to demonstrate how intellectuals who migrate to the Western side of their colonized imagination are prone to employment by the imperial power to inform on their home countries in a manner that confirms conclusions already drawn. Iraqi exiles like Kanan Makiya were used to justify the invasion of Iraq; I wish to argue that this phenomenon, now common, points to the inner logic of imperial domination in the age of globalization. Globalization has decentered the world. I do not write from the site of colony, as Fanon did, nor do I any longer think of myself in exile, as Said did. Neither of those sites—the faraway colony and the alienating exile—is any longer a viable proposition. The world has changed from the time of Fanon, and the condition variously code-named neoliberal, neoconservative, or even multicultural globalization has posited a planetary condition with new modes of domination. One no longer need be in Algeria to be colonized— Harlem, the Bronx, and Newark will do just as well. Contrary to Said, I no longer see the point of being in exile or in diaspora; both these terms alienate and disqualify. Mullah Nasreddin, a proverbial Persian idiot savant, was asked where the center of the universe lay. He pointed to the hook on the ground where his donkey was tied. "There", he said; "there is the center of the universe—and if you don't believe me, go and measure the equidistance from it around the world".

Home is where you hold your horses, hang your hat, and above all raise your voice in defiance and say no to oppression.

1
Brown Skin, White Masks

The black man wants to be white. The white man is desperately trying to achieve the rank of man...As painful as it is for us to have to say this: there is but one destiny for the black man. And it is white.

Frantz Fanon, *Black Skin, White Masks* (1952)

When Americans inaugurated their first African-American president, Barack Hussein Obama, this prompted me to reread Frantz Fanon's *Black Skin, White Masks* and to reflect on what it meant when it was first published, in 1952, and what it means now that a black man is in the White House.

I first read Fanon's masterwork as a youth in Iran in the 1970s. *Post-e Siyah, Suratak-ha-ye Sefid* still sounds more elegiac to my ears than *Black Skin, White Masks*, even more so than its French title, *Peau Noire, Masques Blanc*. Since then I have read and taught Fanon's now furious, now soothing soul book too many times to recall. I call to mind the quote "Don't expect to see any explosion today. It's too early ... or too late".[1] I feel that the span of my own life—the more than half a century of despair and delight that has passed between 1951, when I was born in Iran (two years before the CIA-engineered coup of 1953), and today, some years past the world-changing events of September 11, 2001—is summed up in those opening lines of Fanon's. I grew up thinking it was too early for that explosion; I now live thinking it is too late.

I still have my youthful marginalia in the Persian translation of *Black Skin, White Masks* and my middle-aged comments in its English translation; they show none of the anger I now feel. More than anything else, it is Fanon's calm and composure that commands my attention today:

I honestly think, however, it's time some things were said. Things I'm going to say, not shout. I've long given up shouting...This book should have been written three years ago. But at the time the truths made our blood boil. Today the fever has dropped and truths can be said without having them hurled into people's faces.

They are not intended to endorse zealousness. We are wary of being zealous. Every time we have seen it hatched somewhere it has been an omen of fire, famine, and poverty, as well as contempt for man.[2]

I do my share of shouting in this book. And I too have postponed writing it, as it happens, for three years after I fired the first shots—and still I can only aspire to Fanon's composure. There is also another, rather uncanny, similarity. What probably angered Fanon initially and compelled him into writing *Black Skin, White Masks* was the publication, in 1948, of a self-loathing novella, *I Am a Martinican Woman*, by his fellow Martinican Mayotte Capécia; what impelled me was the publication, in 2003, of a memoir, *Reading Lolita in Tehran*, by Capécia's kindred spirit Azar Nafisi. Why are we always more incensed and troubled by someone who looks and sounds like us than by any other? Is it because we identify with them, or because the world—the white world—identifies us with them? Fanon had the wisdom and patience to wait until he published his *Black Skin, White Masks* to bare his thoughts on *I Am a Martinican Woman*; his scathing critique comprises the second chapter. I can boast no such wisdom and patience, even though I too sat on my review for three years. When Fanon wrote his book he was 27 years old, already battle-fatigued from thinking, reading, writing, and fighting against racism, and on the verge of joining the Algerian National Liberation Front (FLN). It is one thing to be angry and zealous at 27; it is something entirely different at 57. Fanon wrote *Black Skin, White Masks* in Algeria, the site of French colonialism; I write in New York, the commercial capital of a beleaguered empire. The world in Fanon's time was squarely divided between the colonizer and the colonized—North and South, West and East. The world we live in today is no longer thus divided. Certainly, people continue to be colonized apace—"people", as Fanon wrote, "in whom an inferiority complex has taken root, whose local cultural originality has been committed to the grave".[3] The powerful still invade, and occupy, and rule, and plunder, and the weak fight back and yield and defy and die and regroup—inside and outside Algeria. There is an Algeria in Louisiana (the reporting of Hurricane Katrina has made this better known), and the United States now has military bases all over the world—including one off the coast of Algeria.

Though written in an entirely different stage in the long history of colonialism—when the colonizers were white and they flaunted their guns in the streets of the world's Algerias against colored populations who inconvenienced them—Fanon's gut-wrenching text remains all too relevant to a colonialism that has now clothed its naked barbarism and entered a neocolonial stage of globalization, with native informers preaching that imperial adventurism is good for the world, and above all for the people targeted for invasion and salvation. There is a rude and remorseless matter-of-factness about the US-led invasions of Afghanistan and Iraq and a barefaced vulgarity about Israel's prolonged appropriation and occupation of Palestine and its repeated invasions of Lebanon that defies common decency—and yet these atrocities are committed with the straight faces of the morally benevolent. In Fanon's time, the barbarism of French colonialism inspired a Jean-Paul Sartre to create an entire philosophical school out of his rousing condemnation of the French occupation. In my time, the US-led invasion and occupation of Afghanistan and Iraq have produced an Alan Dershowitz and a Michael Ignatieff to justify barbarity and defend torture—not despite the strictures of Western jurisprudence and human-rights discourse but, in fact, through them; and they are still aided by the native informers who are the central concern of this study.

HIS PROPHETIC SOUL

No matter how hard the native informer tries to hide behind a veil of anonymity, conducting himself as though he has always lived and worked in Washington, DC, he enters the capital city only too aware that Fanon has already seen through his pretense—for Fanon is a writer he used to read.

Central to Fanon's view of the colonized mind is the significance of language in the *alienation* of the black person, an ugly colonial process Fanon aimed at reversing via *disalienation*. His primary frame of reference was autobiographical; he dwelled especially on the moment when the Martinican, having gone to France and perfected his French, returns to his homeland: "The black man who has been to the *métropole* is a demigod."[4] With this focus on language at the point where literary and cultural proximity to the white world enables and authorizes the colored person, Fanon anticipates the emergence of the native informer: "All colonized people—in other words, people in whom an inferiority complex has taken root, whose local cultural originality has been committed to the grave—position themselves in relation to the civilizing language, i.e. the metropolitan culture."[5] This remains true of the native informer whose circumstances have improved, as has her command of the colonizers' language (though she still speaks it with an accent). She denigrates any notion of what Fanon calls "local cultural originality", for true literature is of course Western literature, not what she scornfully dismisses, for example as the "so-called Iranian realism". Everything back home lacks originality and is "so-called"—a simulacrum of the truth that can exist only in English (or French, or German and so on). She is very fond of the expression "so-called", for it keeps her afloat where she is most comfortable: on the border of the decidedly undecided, where she can dodge bullets, run for cover, and call the police if someone rudely trespasses onto her property, the English language.

"The more the colonized has assimilated the cultural values of the metropolis," Fanon wrote, "the more he will have escaped the bush. The more he rejects his blackness and the bush, the whiter he will become."[6] By "cultural values" Fanon mostly meant language and literature. But today assimilation into the cultural contours of the metropolis is no longer limited to command of the language (which will always come to a halt at the border of that nasty accent). At this stage of paramount visuality, when people's minds are in their eyes, as it were, the native informer wants "to look like" her masters as well, and the cosmetic industry is there to help. She can bleach her skin, dye her hair blonde, have a quick nose job (of which she speaks very approvingly), maybe even invest in a pair of blue contact lenses. For all practical purposes she can become white—the existential destiny Fanon envisioned for her.

Fanon anticipates our native informer when he reports that "in the colonial army, and particularly in the regiments of the Senegalese soldiers, the 'native' officers are mainly interpreters. They serve to convey to their fellow soldiers the master's orders, and they themselves enjoy a certain status."[7] With the aid of this prototype one can imagine some native compradors still doing their share for the white civilizing mission (*mission civilisatrice*) facilitating others' subjugation to a superior set of symbols. For, again as Fanon further noted, "the more the black Antillean assimilates the French language, the whiter he gets—i.e. the closer he comes to becoming a true human being."[8]

Here, of course, the remnant of an accent becomes seriously problematic, as Fanon notes in regard to the black Antilleans who try in vain to ape the Parisian accent. Whenever Fouad Ajami appears on American television to discuss "the mindset of these Arabs", he never fails to include the phrase "we Americans"; but for the life of him he cannot quite get it through his head that the "A" in "Americans" is closer to a *hamza* than to an *'ayn*. The accent at once alienates, exoticizes, and authorizes him to opine about "these Arabs". Fanon again: "In France they say 'to speak like a book'. In Martinique they say 'to speak like a white man'... He will lock himself in his room and read for hours—desperately working on his diction."[9] But still when the native informer goes for a radio or TV interview the nasty accents accompanies him as an uninvited guest; and for this reason he prefers the silent pages of books and newspapers (*The Wall Street Journal* is a favorite venue) to public appearances—although they do pay awfully well.

Fanon also perceived the rivalry that persists among the colonized as to who is whiter: "We have known, and still know, Antilleans who get annoyed at being taken for Senegalese. It's because the Antillean is more 'évolué' than the African—meaning he is closer to the white man." [10] The same holds true for Iranians in their attitude toward Arabs—for the racialized theories of Orientalists have instructed them that they are "Aryan" and as such of the same superior stock as Europeans; only by some unfortunate accident of geography do they find themselves somewhere between the Arab lands and India. The Orientalists' tales—about Cyrus the Great, Darius the First and Xerxes the Conqueror—continue to haunt them, generation after generation. The racism of Iranians runs viciously deep; they have a horror of being taken for Arab (though they would be delighted to be taken for Italian). The native informer speaks for the white-identified, transnational bourgeoisie that calls her "the voice of the modern Iranian woman"; here, as elsewhere, modernity is white.

The native informer has internalized his white masters' manner of talking to the natives. Fanon pointed out the difference between the ways a white physician talks to white and black patients:

> Twenty European patients come and go: "Please have a seat. Now what's the trouble? What can I do for you today?" In comes a black man or an Arab: "Sit down, old fellow. Not feeling well? Where's it hurting?" When it's not: "You not good?[11]"

Likewise, the native informer considers the niceties of Western literature and culture too refined for the colored populations, though she may even deign to teach them English literature. "When a black man speaks of Marx," Fanon observed, "the first reaction is the following: 'We educated you and now you are turning against your benefactors'."[12] The native informer finds brown people's Marxism crude and outdated and does not consider herself political at all. The black man who dares to speak—as did Fanon, Said, Malcolm X, Léopold Sédar Senghor, and Aimé Césaire—is called anything from passionate to angry, but never "reasonable". He may have a point, he is repeatedly told, but he is so angry he defeats his own purpose. Reason and composure, of course, are white.

WHITE MEN SAVING COLORED WOMEN

In his psychoanalytic unpacking of the colonized mind, Fanon turns his attention to the relationships between "the woman of color and the white man" and "the man of color and the white woman", and in so doing provides an uncannily apt critique of *Reading Lolita in Tehran* more than half a century in advance. Reading Fanon now makes it clear that colonialism really has only a few devices in its ideological arsenal to keep recycling. His actual target is *I Am a Martinican Woman* (*Je suis Martiniquaise*)[13], in which Mayotte Capécia does just what her Iranian counterpart will do decades later: she demonizes colored men and rests the salvation of colored women on the generosity of the white men who will rescue her and her sisters from bondage. And she was almost as celebrated as Nafisi, winning France's *Grand Prix Littéraire des Antilles* in 1949.

The literary merit of *I Am a Martinican Woman* was of course determined by the politics of its vindication of the French colonialists; in the voice of Capécia they had found the perfect ally. "I would have liked to marry, but with a white man," Fanon quotes Capécia's protagonist, "only a colored woman is never quite respectable in the eyes of a white man—even if he loves her, I know well".[14] He continues, "Mayotte loves a white man unconditionally. He is her lord. She asks for nothing, demands nothing, except for a little whiteness in her life."[15] Paramount in the mind and soul of Mayotte is this truth: "I am white; in other words, I embody beauty and virtue, which have never been black. I am the color of day."[16] A little later he argues, "Mayotte is striving for lactification. In a word, the race must be whitened; every woman in Martinique knows this, says this, and reiterates it."[17] Capécia, he notes, "imagines herself a pink-cheeked angel".[18]

Turning his attention to Capécia's next novella, *The White Negress*, Fanon notes that every black man she describes "is either a scumbag or a grinning *Y a bon Banania*".[19] And he adds these premonitory words: "Moreover, and this is already an omen, we can safely say that Mayotte Capécia has turned her back to her island. In both books only one course is left for her heroine, i.e. leave. This island of blacks is decidedly cursed."[20] Nafisi, too, has moved to the Paris of her time, Washington, and has done much better than her Martinican predecessor in courting the powerful—even while talking about "this strange institution (in Derrida's phrase) 'called literature'".[21]

WHITE WOMEN SAVING COLORED MEN

Fanon balances his analysis of the colored woman and the white man with a psychoanalysis of the colored man's fantasies of the white woman (but not vice versa): "I want to be recognized not as black, but as white. But—and this is the form of recognition that Hegel never described—who better than the white woman to bring this about? By loving me, she proves to me that I am worthy of the white love. I am loved like a white man. I am a white man."[22] This is as true in the erotic zone as in the political, where the native informer enjoys the approving gaze of the white woman cast upon his services in the imperial capital—I speak with your president, advise your vice-president and the Congress, and appear regularly on national TV. For the native informer the famous salvo with which Nietzsche opens *Beyond Good and Evil*—"Suppose truth is a woman, what then?"—takes on a racial tinge: truth becomes a white woman who will mother his children and breed the black out of his posterity. She will make their future bright—and white.

Having dealt with Capécia's *I Am a Martinican Woman* (as well as Abdoulaye Sadji's *Nini*), Fanon now turns his attention to the other side of the pathology via a similarly critical reading of the autobiographical 1947 novel *Un homme pareil aux autres (A Man Same as Others)* by the French Guyanese poet and novelist René Maran (1887–1960).[23] In psychoanalyzing Maran's protagonist, Jean Veneuse, Fanon works his way toward what the French psychoanalyst Germaine Guex has designated *the abandonment neurosis (la névrose d'abandon)*. He perceives the quagmire in which the black man finds himself caught—"incapable of integrating, incapable of going unnoticed, he starts conversing with the dead or at least the absent...[with] Marcus Aurelius, Joinville, Pascal, Pérez Galdós, Rabindranath Tagore". [24] Above all he is "anxious", "uneasy with his body" [25]—which thus becomes the locus of the white woman's saving grace.

Even at the early stage that Fanon analyzes him, the sexual pathology of the native informer is positively psychotic. Jean Veneuse is reminiscent of Mustafa Sa'eed in Tayeb Salih's *Season of Migration to the North* (1966), but he has his criminal urges far more under control, and his softer demeanor thus makes him more palatable to whites. As Fanon typifies him, "Veneuse is black, he is a solitary creature. He's a thinker. And when a woman attempts to flirt with him: 'You're dealing with an old bear! Be careful, my dear!'"[26] Fanon pulls no punches, for much more than a psychoanalysis his book is an act of liberation inspired by Marx's notion that there has been enough interpretation of the world and it is now time to change it. Thus he offers a sharp and edgy diagnosis of the would-be native informer's trapped consciousness: "Forgive us the expression, but Jean Veneuse is the man to be slaughtered. We shall do our best... here is our black man 'who through his intelligence and hard work has hoisted himself to the level of European thought and culture', but is incapable of escaping his race."[27] Both Veneuse and Sa'eed strive toward the same goal, to overcome their race—Veneuse by coupling with a white woman, Sa'eed by murdering her. In both, the native informer has invested everything good yet unattainable in a figment of his own imagination. Same pathology, different outcomes.

"You have nothing in common with a real Negro," the brother of the white woman to whom Veneuse is attracted tells him, "you are not black; you are very, very dark."[28] Although, as Fanon reminds us, "we know that historically the Negro found guilty of sleeping with a white woman was castrated".[29] This is not the moment of Veneuse's castration. Nor is it the moment when Fanon, pinpointing the black man's lack of self-esteem (Veneuse is "a neurotic", "one of those intellectuals who position themselves solely at an abstract level", and above all "ugly. He is black"[30]) narrows in on the abandonment neurosis. Fanon gears his conclusions in a different direction:

> We would like to think we have discouraged any attempt to connect the failure of Jean Veneuse with the amount of melanin in his epidermis. The sexual myth—the obsession with white flesh—conveyed by alienated minds must no longer be an obstacle to understanding the question. In no way must my color be felt as a stain from the moment the black man accepts the split imposed by the Europeans, there is no longer any respite;

and

> [quoting from Claude Nordey's *L'homme de couleur/The Colored Man* (1939)]
> from that moment on, isn't it understandable that he will try to elevate himself to the white man's level? To elevate himself

into the range of colors to which he has attributed a kind of hierarchy?[31]

Fanon's response to Nordey's question is an emphatic *"no!"* "We shall see that another solution is possible. It implies restructuring the world."[32]

Fanon's examination of the pathological disposition of the colored man toward the white woman posits the paradoxical erotics at the root of the politics of domination—anticipating what would later happen, for example, in Baghdad's Abu Ghraib prison. a short time into the US-led occupation of Iraq. Absent from Fanon's analysis is the white woman's stance toward the colored man—for example, PFC Lynndie England's attitude toward the male prison inmates whom she forced to strip naked and then mocked with sexually explicit gestures while she and PFC Charles A. Graner Jr. (her boyfriend and the father of the child she was carrying) took snapshots of them. When, in the course of an interview, I compared England with Azar Nafisi, the entire platoon of Nafisi's neoconservative friends attacked me. But, in making that comparison, I was referring to Fanon's insight that the psychosis between the colored woman and white man does a double somersault in the white woman's fantasy of the colored man's tortured and humiliated body. These complementary fantasies are the two sides of the same delusional coin. While Nafisi, the native informer, carries out the fantasy according to the classical prognosis of Fanon, England, the prison guard, reverses the fantasy, forcing the colored man back into his humiliated position. Both Nafisi and England have the same function: to denigrate and humiliate the colored man (the site of resistance to imperial domination), one via a literary narrative that ridicules and humiliates him, the other by stripping him, putting a leash around his neck, and pointing scornfully at his genitalia.

THE BLACK AND THE ARAB

As Fanon anticipates in Capécia a future generation of native informers including Nafisi, Hirsi Ali, and Irshad Manji, he also anticipates what we may call the emergence of the Arab as the next African and the Muslim as the new Jew. This he accomplishes via a critical dialogue with a famous study of colonialism that had just appeared, O. Mannoni's *Prospero and Caliban: The Psychology of Colonization* (1950), and its central thesis of a "dependency complex". Fanon takes Mannoni severely to task for his notion that the germ of an inferiority complex is latent in the colonized person from childhood[33], stressing the colonial—i.e. economic—condition behind this assumption of inferiority. Mannoni, while suggesting that something servile was present in the colonial subject even before the European arrived, also argues that "European civilization and its best representative are not, for instance, responsible for colonial racialism; that is the work of petty officials, small traders and colonials who have toiled much without great success". Fanon contradicts him forcefully: "Yes, European civilization and its agents of the highest caliber are responsible for colonial racism."[34]

Half a century after Fanon's empowering words, conditions at the heart of the American empire confirm his diagnosis. Alan Dershowitz, one of Harvard's most prominent professors of law, has offered a legal defense for the torture of Arabs and Muslims; another Harvard scholar, Michael Ignatieff (now the leader of Canada's liberal party), has seconded Dershowitz's call for torture employing a human-rights defense; Nafisi has used Western literature to denigrate Iranian society and culture; and Salman Rushdie's rampage against Islam and Muslims has found support in the highest echelons of the European and American literary intelligentsia. In the *Washington Post*, Anne Applebaum praises Hirsi Ali's 2007 memoir, *Infidel*, as "something more than an ordinary autobiography" because it is written in "the tradition of Frederick Douglass or even John Stuart Mill".[35] Forgetting for the moment the irony of equating a revolutionary black American with a British colonialist, Douglass and Mill are not anything like the "petty officials" and "small traders" of Mannoni's West; how can their names be invoked to praise the work of someone who admitted lying in order to secure political asylum in Holland,[36] has been accused of plagiarism,[37] has scandalized Europe, has fled to the bosom of neoconservatism in Washington DC, and became the willing and well-paid mouthpiece for the European and American Islamophobia?

Racism is not "an exception to" but "the rule of" European colonialism, and what has promoted and sustained it is not any innate inferiority on the part of "the natives" (thus nativized) but its promotion by the best "Western civilization", as invoked by Hirsi Ali, Nafisi, Rushdie, and so on. Until and unless the cutting edge of European racism is turned inward against itself, Europeans will remain blind to it. Fanon implicates the entirety of Western civilization in its global barbarities by quoting Aimé Césaire: "And then one fine day the bourgeoisie is awakened by a terrific boomerang effect, the gestapos are busy, the prisons fill up, the torturers standing around the racks invent, refine, discuss."[38] Their mutual point is that when the victims of European barbarism were in faraway Asia, Africa, and Latin America the European *Hochkultur* did not mind; only once its wrath turned inward toward the Europeans (especially Jewish Europeans) themselves did they begin to wonder where the monster had come from. In Césaire's formulation, "they tolerated that Nazism before it was inflicted on them", he charges "that they absolved it, shut their eyes to it, because until then, it had been applied only to non-European peoples; that they have cultivated that Nazism, that they are responsible for it, and that before engulfing the whole edifice of Western, Christian civilization in its reddened waters, it oozes, seeps and trickles from every crack".[39]

Dismissing any inborn proclivity to servitude, Fanon then points to a subcategorized group of hidden victims—the subaltern of the subaltern, an underclass of the colonized people not even categorized yet:

> How many times have I been stopped in broad daylight by the police, who took me for an Arab, and when they discovered my origins, they hastily apologized: "We know full well a Martinican is different from an Arab." I would protest violently, but I was told: "You don't know them." Truly, Monsieur Mannoni, you are wrong: "European civilization and its best representatives are not responsible for colonial racism?"[40]

Fanon's point is the economic basis of both colonial domination and the colonized mentality—he will have none of the pre-existing inferiority that Mannoni suggests: "If we add that many Europeans set off for the colonies because they can get rich over there in a very short time...you will have grasped the psychology of the man who produces the 'feeling of inferiority' in the native."[41] By turning his attention to the Arab who is even more tyrannized by the European than he himself, Fanon anticipates a future point when the Arab will emerge as the new African, the Muslim as the new Jew, and brown as the new black; and he pre-empts the need to fetishize any one of these color-coded conditions of domination, arguing instead for global understanding of the manner in which capital keeps reinventing its cultures of domination. It is under that recodified condition of coloniality—when *Negritude* is codified but *Arabness* and *Muslimhood* is not—that our native informers and the services they provide need to be placed and understood.

THE MUSLIM IS THE NEW JEW

What today's native informers have made clear is that the white imagination has now recodified the color of its chronic racism. The Arab and the Muslim have replaced the black and the Jew as the demonic "other" of the white Christian self. During the US presidential election of 2008, racist Americans loudly proclaimed that Obama was black; they claimed he was Muslim and believed he was an Arab.

As Arabs and Muslims emerge as the new demons, especially in the aftermath of 9/11, a panoply of Iranian, Arab, Pakistani, and other Muslim expatriate academics and intellectuals has taken full advantage of the hostility toward Muslims and Muslim-majority countries to reinforce the perception of these societies as constitutionally degenerate and direly in need of emancipatory intervention. This conclusion has been at times explicit, as in the writings of Fouad Ajami[42] and Kanan Makiya[43] during the build-up to the invasion of Iraq; at times implicit, as in the cases of Nafisi and Hirsi Ali. But the tone and texture of the development are the same: Either way, these comprador intellectuals have been given unprecedented forums by the North American and Western European media in which to paint a picture of Muslim societies that tallies perfectly with what the needs of US propaganda are, thereby justifying the country's post-9/11 imperial projects.

Behind this picture of Muslim societies as irredeemably backward lay the imperial desire to dominate the world without a convincing ideology of hegemony. In a 2004 essay, "Tentacles of Rage: The Republican Propaganda Mill, a Brief History",[44] Lewis Lapham begins with a question from the American historian Richard Hofstadter (1916–70): "When, in all our history, has anyone with ideas so bizarre, so archaic, so self-confounding, so remote from the basic American consensus, ever got so far?"[45] He continues with a piercing account of the various facets of a propaganda machinery that, ever since the civil rights movement of the 1960s, has been paving the way to the post-9/11 triumph of a neoconservatism bent on global domination. At around the same time, in *Colossus: The Price of America's Empire*,[46] the Scottish historian Niall Ferguson posited American military, economic, and even pop-cultural imperialism as "the Imperialism of anti-Imperialism" and showed how, in the annals of American history, "liberty" has usually stood for "empire".

The central function of the native informers, meanwhile, has been to facilitate this white supremacist replacement of a black demon with a brown one, a Jew with a Muslim. It was evident during the *Jyllands-Posten* Muhammad-cartoons controversy of 2005–06, when Salman Rushdie and a band of like-minded native informers used these events to warn Europeans and Americans that they now faced a threat as dangerous as fascism—posed by a scattered band of corrupt and incompetent Muslim states and a massively poor and disenfranchised Muslim community scattered throughout Europe and North America. What is paramount in this incident (as I will argue in Chapter 3) is the transmutation of Europe's historical anti-Semitism into an equally widespread and tenacious Islamophobia—with self-loathing Muslim native informers facilitating the transition.

THE NATIVE INFORMER AT LARGE

For the American imperial project to claim global validity it needs the support of native informers and comprador intellectuals with varying accents to their speech, their prose, and politics. Supported only by white men and women, the project would not have the same degree of narrative authority. But accents from targeted cultures and climes Orientalize, exoticize, and corroborate all at the same time; they accentuate that supremely self-alienating moment when by offering their services native informers authorize and authenticate the dominant accent—which no longer hears its own imperial accent.

The project that has occasioned these native informers is of course nothing new in the history of European colonialism and American imperialism. From the scramble for Africa to the conquest of Asia to the plundering of Latin America, the white man's burden has included the necessity of persuading "the natives" that they can never be the agents of their own history. The project of Orientalism, as Said has diagnosed it, was instrumental in manufacturing this consent. But the aggressive globalization of imperial conquest has, if anything, increased the importance of the ideological machinery that works to make the conquest of the world appear as a humane project, a liberation. Next to national-security interests, human rights and women's rights in particular are now routinely cited as the principal objectives of American imperial interventions. The role of Hirsi Ali, Nafisi, Irshad Manji. and their ilk is to speak on behalf of such rights as integral to the humanitarian mission at the heart of American imperialism. Offering, in English for the American and

European market, a fierce critique of women's rights in Iran (Nafisi) or genital mutilation in Africa (Hirsi Ali) or gay and lesbian rights in Islam across the board (Irshad Manji)[47] places the authority to right these wrongs in the hands of the foreign readers and their elected officials, rather than the societies affected. At a New York City event in October 2004 honoring an Iranian women's-rights activist, to which a wide spectrum of guests were invited, I found on every table a copy of *Reading Lolita in Tehran* next to a postcard bearing a picture of a battered African woman and a message demanding intervention on behalf of her and women like her, to sign and send off to Secretary of State Colin Powell. This was three years into the US-led carnage in Afghanistan and a year into the criminal occupation of Iraq.

The best way to extend Fanon's revolutionary legacy into the contingencies of our own time is to remain awake to the way the ideological machinery of beleaguered capital keeps reinventing itself. Today, in the age of cross-coded multiculturalism, capital needs newer forms of domination, facilitated by homeless, soulless native informers who have taken over the work that the racist Orientalists once performed. What we are witnessing today is simply a more advanced stage of colonialism, reflecting a more advanced condition of capitalism in its globalized stage, with newer forms of domination in need of a renewed ideological language. It is thus absolutely imperative that we do not counter-fetishize any particular color-coded mode of ideological domination—black or brown, Jew or Muslim—as a target of moral assassination. Capital, in the end, is color-blind and gender-neutral. It wants to produce cheaply and sell massively to the widest possible market, and it could not care less who buys, who sells, who profits, and who suffers the consequences of this treacherous cycle. The service that the native informers provide to the imperialist project is just another disposable commodity in that cycle, like a roll of toilet paper—use it, discard it, and leave.

2
On Comprador Intellectuals

We must at present do our best to form a class who may be interpreters between us and the millions whom we govern; a class of persons, Indian in blood and color, but English in taste, in opinions, in morals, and in intellect.

—Thomas B. Macaulay, "Minute on Education" (1835)

An Eastern race well versed in Western culture and profoundly in sympathy with Western ideals will be established in the Orient. Furthermore, a Jewish state will inevitably fall under the control of American Jews who will work out, along Jewish lines, American ideals and American civilization.

—William Yale, US State Department (1919)

In those days he was called a "house nigger". And that's what we call him today, because we've still got some house niggers running around here.

—Malcolm X (1963)

Just as, hidden in the self-loathing colonized mind that Fanon diagnosed, seethed the future *native informer*, so did the defiant *exilic intellectual* whom Edward Said saw as the locus of dissent at the heart of the empire. In his 1993 Reith Lectures, published the next year as *Representations of the Intellectual*, Said proposed this exilic intellectual as the savior of an otherwise lost cause. In his 1987 diagnostic essay *The Last Intellectuals*, Russell Jacoby had written the obituary of the public intellectual in the United States.[1] Said, in response, detected a critical character that had escaped Jacoby's notice at the margins of the American metropolis:

> While it is an actual condition, exile is also for my purposes a metaphorical condition ... Even intellectuals who are lifelong members of a society can, in a manner of speaking, be divided into insiders and outsiders: those on the one hand who belong fully to the society as it is, who flourish in it without an overwhelming sense of dissonance or dissent, those who can be called yea-sayers; and on the other hand, the nay-sayers, the individuals at odds with their society and therefore outsiders and exiles so far as privileges, power, and honors are concerned.[2]

Said's exilic intellectual (clearly a self-projection) is never at home anywhere, always opposing the arguments that serve power. His concept contains references to a range of intellectuals as diverse as Theodore Adorno, Eqbal Ahmad, Noam Chomsky, and, of course, Said himself, all solitary souls rebelling against the power that seeks to silence or assimilate them.

This exilic condition does not refer to an actual separation from a homeland (Adorno from Germany, Ahmad from Pakistan, Said from Palestine) but to a critical angle on power and a defiant character ill at ease with any communal claim on his or her loyalty. Chomsky is thus an exile in his own homeland. The prototype is a sort of amphibian character who has left the colonial site of his upbringing for the presumed center of capital ("presumed" because capital no longer has a center) to dismantle its ideological edifice and subvert its claim to political legitimacy. As a Fifth Column, or a Trojan Horse, the exilic intellectual assumes the guise of a migrant laborer, a passenger in transit, a homeless vagabond, fooling the customs by smuggling subversive ideas through gates, pretending to innocence while carrying a backpack full of explosive ideas.

FROM EXILIC TO COMPRADOR INTELLECTUAL

In the shadow of Said's exilic intellectual, however, has always lurked a parasite called the comprador intellectual. In his reflections on the various manners of Africa, Kwame Anthony Appiah, locates this character in a "relatively small, Western-style, Western-trained group of writers and thinkers, who mediate the trade in cultural commodities of world capitalism at the periphery".[3] Despite its usefulness, that limited definition of comprador intellectual is much in need of reconsideration. For Appiah, the idea is very much contingent on a nebulous category called "the West", and it operates between a binary center-and-periphery that is no longer valid.

The Portuguese word comprador dates from 1840 and refers to a Chinese agent engaged by a European business interest in China to oversee its native employees and to act as an intermediary in its business affairs. Later, it was extended to refer to any native servant in the service of a colonial commercial interest—someone "employed by Europeans, in India and the East", according to the *Oxford English Dictionary*, "to purchase necessaries and keep the household accounts: a house-steward." The concept carries an obvious ideological subtext that becomes crucially functional in mobilizing public sentiment in support of colonial and imperial projects. The comprador intellectual is a cultural broker, a commissioned operator, a "ten-percenter" paid to facilitate cultural domination and political pacification. He has some familiarity with the dominating culture, which he serves out of self-interest (not conviction), he speaks its language (with an accent), and by virtue of the proximity he seeks to power becomes abusive of his own compatriots.

But Appiah's characterization falls short of the nature and disposition of the category. Far sharper is Malcolm X's designation of the functional equivalent of the comprador intellectual in his "Message to the Grass Roots", delivered in Detroit on November 10, 1963:

> There were two kinds of slaves. There was the house Negro and the field Negro. The house Negroes—they lived in the house with master, they dressed pretty good, they ate good 'cause they ate his food—what he left. They lived in the attic or the basement, but still they lived near the master; and they loved their master more than the master loved himself. They would give their life to save the master's house quicker than the master would. The house Negro, if the master said, "We got a good house here," the house Negro would say, "Yeah, we got a good house here." Whenever the master said "we", he said "we". That's how you can tell a house Negro.[4]

Malcolm X has moved the figure of the comprador intellectual from the periphery—the field—into the normative universe of the master. His figure is more dialectical than Appiah's, for he moves back and forth between the field and the house—informing and/or misinforming the master about the nature and disposition of those in the field. The master takes the house slave for the authentic thing, while the house slave himself believes he is serving the master best by informing him about the field slaves—when in fact they are both delusional, caught in a dialectic of reciprocity in which they are abusing each other without knowing it. This is Malcolm X's superior insight.

In the context of French domination in North Africa, Albert Memmi offered an equally accurate diagnosis of the malady in his *Colonizer and the Colonized* (1957):

> The situation of the Jewish population—eternally hesitant candidates refusing assimilation—can be viewed in a similar light.

Their constant and very justifiable ambition is to escape from their colonized condition, an additional burden in an already oppressive status. To that end, they endeavor to resemble the colonizer in the frank hope that they may cease to consider them different from him. Hence their efforts to forget the past, to change collective habits, and their enthusiastic adoption of Western language, culture and customs. But if the colonizer does not always openly discourage these candidates to develop that resemblance he never permits them to attain it either. Thus they live in painful and constant ambiguity. Rejected by the colonizer they share in part the physical conditions of the colonized and have a communion of interest with him; on the other hand, they reject the values of the colonized as belonging to a decayed world from which they eventually hope to escape. The recently assimilated place themselves in considerable superior position to the average colonizer. They push a colonial mentality to excess, display proud disdain for the colonized and continually show off their rank, which often belies a vulgar brutality and avidity. Still too impressed by their privileges, they savor them and defend with fear and harshness; and when colonization is imperiled, they provide it with its most dynamic defenders, its shock troops, and sometimes instigators.[5]

Memmi's analysis is not limited to the Jewish population; he has diagnosed the overwhelming power of white supremacist hegemony. Rabindranath Tagore's description, in his famous novel *Gora* (1910), of the English-identified Bengali comprador intellectuals halfway around the globe from North Africa perfectly matches Memmi's. The comprador intellectual is a by-product of colonialism, not a character trait of any given culture.

Said's exilic intellectual defies the power relation operative in his domain, whereas Appiah's comprador intellectual is subservient to it. The one has migrated to the heart of darkness, where the empire manages its domestic and foreign affairs; the other has stayed behind and provides his services on the colonial site. But if we place Malcolm X's analysis between Said's and Appiah's, we come to a far more accurate conception of both the exilic and the comprador intellectuals, because each is involved in a dialectical traffic between the center and the periphery (thus collapsing both into one world). Malcolm X has a dynamic conception of political manipulation, social mobility, and the economic underpinnings of power:

If the master's house caught on fire, the house Negro would fight harder to put the blaze out than the master would. If the master got sick, the house Negro would say, "What's the matter, boss, we sick?" We sick! He identified himself with his master more than his master identified with himself. And if you came to the house Negro and said, "Let's run away, let's escape, let's separate," the house Negro would look at you and say, "Man, you crazy. What you mean, separate? Where is there a better house than this? Where can I wear better clothes than this? Where can I eat better food than this?"[6]

Malcolm X's house Negro and Said's exilic intellectual are two sides of the same analytical coin, one serving the white master and the other revolting against him.

Just as Said's exilic intellectual may be in actual or metaphoric exile, the comprador intellectual can actually be in the field or metaphorically there, or alternatively, he can move into the house. Whichever way, he is always located on the side of power. The advantage of Said and Malcolm X's combination of insights is that, in an increasingly amorphous and boundary-less world, it no longer requires us to divide intellectuals along a fictitious center-periphery axis. The actual location of the comprador intellectual on that axis has become increasingly tenuous. In a 1997 essay on the same phenomenon as it relates to the Palestinian predicament, Joseph Massad maintains that the events of 1967 facilitated the emergence of a new breed of comprador intellectuals.[7] "The Arab defeat in the 1967 war announced the retreat of a period of secular revolutionary thinking, with the Camp David Accord of 1978 and 1979 dealing it a final coup de grace, giving way to a new crop of thinkers: Islamists and realist-pragmatist."[8] The latter are Massad's Palestinian comprador intellectuals:

This transformation wherein Palestinian intellectuals who previously opposed the occupation, PLO concessions, and US hegemony, but now support, wittingly or unwittingly, all three, is not a unique transformation. It would seem that like their Soviet counterparts who rushed to trade in their communism for realist pragmatism upon the fall of the Soviet state, or their Latin American counterparts who, like Fernando Henrique Cardoso, traded in their dependency theory approach for positions of power ... Palestinian intellectuals, attuned to the exigencies of political power and the benefits that could accrue to them from it, traded in their national liberation goals for pro-Western pragmatism.[9]

Massad's comprador intellectuals could be in or out of Palestine, within the 1948 or 1967 borders or out in the diaspora. Where they reside does not really matter; they no longer have a fixed location on what Appiah calls "the periphery", and thus the whole axis of center-periphery reveals itself as misplaced and fictive.

THE COMPRADOR INTELLECTUAL MOVES IN

Comprador intellectuals have always been close to the mobilized center of power—which in this rapidly globalizing world might be just about anywhere but is increasingly at the center of empire. In a 2003 essay, "The Native Informant",[10] Adam Shatz has done a service by placing a prominent example of the comprador intellectual at the heart of the mobilized Imperium: Fouad Ajami, who lives and works in Washington DC. Ajami advises high-ranking US officials and regularly works as a media pundit when American imperialism flexes its muscles around the Muslim world. Ajami does not perform his compradorial services from Southern Lebanon; he has moved so deeply into the normative imagination of the imperial power that he does not quite hear the macabre humor when he says, "We Americans ought to understand how the mind of these Arabs works!"

This question has in recent years assumed an intriguing turn with a writer who publishes sensational tirades against Islam and Muslims under the pseudonym Ibn Warraq. That readers have no clue as to who or where he or she really is (Ibn is Arabic for "the son of", but a pseudonym need not be truthful) beautifully demonstrates how tenuous the physical location of the comprador intellectual can be; what is important is the move to the symbolic center of power. In a series of highly provocative titles (including *Why I Am Not a Muslim, The Quest for the Historical Muhammad*), this character has launched flamboyant attacks on the verities of the Islamic religion, the prophet, and the sacred Islamic text. His compradorial courtship of anti-Muslim sentiment is exceptionally valuable to the "clash of civilizations" proposition.

Precisely because he is dislocated, he demands attention. In book after book, Warraq takes a perverse pleasure in recounting the most offensive assertions about Islam that European Orientalists (Dante, Hobbes, Voltaire, Hume, Gibbon, Carlyle) have uttered over the years. He suffers from a severe case of Rushdie syndrome, trying to "up the ante" in his ever more perverse assaults on his own ancestral faith. That a book like *Why I Am Not a Muslim*[11] resurrects a long-dead manifestation of Orientalism is not really much of a problem. The political economy that once necessitated Orientalism as a system of colonial knowledge production has long since generated a new propaganda machinery, under whose modus operandi Warraq's obscenities have to be understood

The case of Azar Nafisi bears on this same question of location. Her memoir *Reading Lolita in Tehran* recounts how she has saved the souls of seven students in Tehran (and with them, symbolically, the rest of Iran) by inviting them into her home to teach them Vladimir Nabokov's novel and "other masterpieces of western literature". She did live in Tehran. She subsequently moved to the United States, and she now lives in the vicinity of the American capital and teaches as an adjunct at the Paul H. Nitze School of Advanced International Studies at Johns Hopkins University in Baltimore. (At the time she was writing her memoir she was reporting directly to its dean, Paul Wolfowitz.) The location Nafisi claims by virtue of her bestselling book is, in fact, fictitious: it purports to be Tehran, but the book was actually written in Washington DC.

We can no longer automatically place comprador intellectuals at the periphery of any center, nor indeed at the center of any periphery; they are everywhere, because they are nowhere in particular, and they are nowhere in particular because they simply try to keep close to the mobilized center of power. "How do you define your own status in this country?" one interviewer asked Azar Nafisi—"exile, émigré, a citizen of the world?" She answered, "I would like to think of my own status as what you called 'citizen of the world' or a 'citizen of a portable world'"[12]—which in this situation, one could argue, suggests a homeless mind, a "carpetbagger", a very doctrinaire sort of intellectual.

Given the rapid deterioration of the smokescreen historically separating the domestic and foreign abuses of labor by capital that goes by the code name "globalization", we can no longer sustain a distance between a presumed center and a projected periphery in the amorphous operation of capital. As a result, the comprador intellectual needs to be categorically reconsidered as a type— thematically extended, functionally globalized, and physically relocated to any place the emerging empire seeks to sustain the operation of capital. The type has become more bourgeois in style and training, no longer simply mediating the trade of cultural commodities but in fact manufacturing them in such a way as to facilitate the operation of globalized capital and its corresponding empire-building projects.

RETHINKING THE COMPRADORIAL

If, based on these examples—which can be extended with many others (including V. S. Naipaul, Salman Rushdie, Dinesh D'Souza)— we shift the emphasis from the physical location to the place that the comprador intellectual imaginatively resides, then the entire category assumes a significance beyond the classical definition of colored individuals in ideological servitude to white masters. Through the opening up of horizons, we can radically recast these intellectuals according to the newly-globalized service they now provide to power.

As a case in point, consider the *New York Times*' Thomas Friedman, who is fond of signing his name to his columns from one troubled part of the world after another. In his ideological services to the American empire he is all but identical to Fouad Ajami, Dinesh D'Souza, Azar Nafisi—they all think alike and speak the same language, and they often endorse one another. The category can become perfectly color-blind, because capital and its changing ideologies are ultimately color-blind.

The word comprador comes from the Spanish and Portuguese comprar, "to buy", and thus entails the specific function of facilitating the flow of capital through trade. Its original meaning, "a native servant employed by Europeans in the East", refers to a specific period in the history of capital when it divided the world between white masters and colored natives along an East-West axis no longer valid in a world of globalized capitalism and 24-hour trading. The world today is more than ever divided between the overwhelming majority who are abused by capital and the very few who are its beneficiaries. The defining function of the comprador intellectuals is to shore up that relation of commerce to power. Birthplace, nationality, religion, creed, and color are all irrelevant. Capital will use whatever and whoever is convenient for each particular time, place and situation.

At the same time, we may note that the emergence of this comprador character in the shadow of Said's exilic intellectual coincides with a particularly anti-intellectual episode in contemporary American history. As intellectuals such as Ajami, Nafisi, Warraq, and Rushdie are set loose during George W. Bush's "War on Terror" to discredit their own culture, they leave a void in the public space for a far more radical eradication of the defiant public intellectual—a task most recently performed by (among others) Mark Lilla, who in a series of essays originally published in *The New York Review of Books* and *The Times Literary Supplement* and subsequently collected between hard covers as *The Reckless Mind* launched an attack against dissenting voices raised in objection to the imperial terrors perpetrated by the United States against the world at large. Close attention to Lilla's anti-intellectual diatribes[13] will help clarify the comprador intellectual's transit beyond color and creed into the normative paradigms of the belligerent empire.

Lilla goes through a gamut of European intellectuals, from Martin Heidegger and Karl Schmidt to Walter Benjamin and Alexander Kojève and on down to Michel Foucault and Jacques Derrida, who have in his judgment committed some political atrocity or other; the reckless of his title has condoned fascism, communism, or "countless national liberation movements" (for Lilla they are all one and the same) and has portrayed "Western liberal democracies" in diabolical terms.[14] In his systematically anti-intellectual defense of the vacuous cause of a twentieth-century "Western liberal democracy" that he never subjects to critical inquiry, not once does Lilla utter a word about the global atrocities of classical European colonialism or of present-day imperial American warmongering. For him it is a given that only reckless intellectuals and demagogues would take issue with "Western liberal democracies", or with what he calls, in jest, "the tyranny of capital, of imperialism, of bourgeois conformity". In Lilla's eyes, "the facts were rarely in dispute; they were apparent to anyone who read the newspapers and had a sense of moral proportion". Those facts would, of course, appear in newspaper stories written by embedded journalists. That "sense of moral proportion" apparently does not apply to the torture chambers in Bagram Air Base and Abu Ghraib, or to the elaborate arguments in their defense that Alan Dershowitz and Michael Ignatieff have taken straight from the "Western liberal democracies".

What is most astonishing about Lilla's attack on European public intellectuals is that it coincides with one of the most vicious periods of American imperial hubris, of violence perpetrated against weak and colored peoples in violation of international laws. This anti-intellectualism (so definitive of American cultural history that it was recognized by as early an observer as Alexis de Tocqueville), denouncing any public figure who dares to speak out against US military thuggery around the world, is essential to the function of comprador intellectuals and native informers at the service of the predatory empire. Lilla suffers from a transcontinental ahistoricism that leaps easily from ancient Greece to contemporary Iraq. He traverses the distance between Plato and Saddam Hussein without the slightest hesitation or concern—and with a single-minded determination to discredit any public intellectual who has ever taken a public stand against any atrocity committed by the "Western liberal democracies".

After a volume's worth of gossip about Martin Heidegger and Hannah Arendt's love affair, Walter Benjamin's extramarital indiscretions, Michel Foucault's homosexuality, and other equally irrelevant aspects of these prominent intellectuals' private lives, Lilla turns to Plato and Dionysius in order to issue a verdict against a few minor dinosaurs, completely ignoring—and thus exonerating—the major source of violence in the world, the military might of the United States. His attacks have an uncanny similarity to the smear campaigns now endemic to presidential electioneering. Do we really care about Foucault's sexual preferences or Sartre's indiscretions? Is Arendt disqualified from speaking about Auschwitz because as a student she had an affair with her professor? Do these entirely private aspects of these public intellectuals' lives discredit their principled stands against criminal atrocities around the globe? Of course not.

Equally puzzling is Lilla's equation of Heidegger's Nazi affiliation with Foucault's anti-fascism. But we may solve the puzzle when we realize that via such ahistorical and illogical links Lilla discredits any political concern on the part of public intellectuals. In the course of equating National Socialism with every other national-liberation movement, he remains under the delusion that he is not taking a political position himself—that he is not placing his laptop squarely at the service of a predatory empire. "Dionysius is our contemporary," he writes,[15] and in Saddam Hussein and Ayatollah Khomeini he finds reincarnations of that terrible tyrant. In a moment of naked indiscretion he declares, "The harems and food-tasters of ancient times are indeed gone but their places have been taken by propaganda ministers and revolutionary guards, drug barons and Swiss bankers. The tyrant has survived. The problem of Dionysius is as old as creation."[16] Texas ranchers without a "harem and food-tasters" to shame them, with CNN and Fox News functioning like "propaganda outlets" and a mercenary army to act as their "revolutionary guards," do not cross Lilla's mind.

What, then, are the subjects of a predatory empire to do when faced with the criminal monstrosities of a George W. Bush or an Ariel Sharon—or, for that matter, of a Saddam Hussein, an Ayatollah Khomeini, an Osama bin Laden? Are they to remain silent, to implicitly endorse Bush's "liberation" of Afghanistan and Iraq as a way of spreading "Western liberal democracy"? Would that exempt one, in Lilla's view, from the transgressions of a reckless mind? What about those caught in the snare of tyrants—should they not utter a word? And what, exactly, is Lilla doing himself? Is his own public-intellectual-denouncing text a work of pure, politics-free philosophical speculation?

Had Heidegger had an affair with Arendt but no affiliation with the Nazis, or vice versa, would he have passed Lilla's test as a responsible philosopher? How could one equate Karl Schmitt's visceral anti-Semitism and Walter Benjamin's despair at the terror looming over European Jews, which could not but have included a passing attraction to messianic politics? And what did Benjamin's love affair with the Latvian intellectual Asja Lacis have to do with his turn to Marxism? What did Alexandre Kojève's intellectual grand-fathering of a triumphalist theorist like Francis Fukuyama have to do with Michel Foucault's politics, or Foucault's homosexuality with his position on power? When Lilla comes to Jacques Derrida, having failed to find any "dirt" on him he simply expresses utter contempt for French philosophers as public intellectuals. His greatest disdain, however, is for the American academic left, which in his estimation has misunderstood the paragons of the European engagé philosophy and concocted a postmodernism for which he does not hide his contempt.

The moral of Lilla's story is that "whoever takes it upon himself to write an honest intellectual history of twentieth-century Europe will need a strong stomach."[17] Lilla suffers gastroenterological distress because European intellectuals have sacrificed the cause of *pure* philosophy to *impure* political engagement. He expresses his judgment via a binary opposition between Sartre (the Indian of his personal political Western) and Raymond Aron (the cowboy):

In his influential Plaidoyer pour les intellectuels, texts of lectures given in 1965, Sartre portrayed the intellectual as a left-wing Jeanne d'Arc who stands for what is essentially human against the inhuman forces of economic and political "power", and also against those reactionary cultural forces, including traitorous fellow writers, whose work "objectively" supports the modern tyrant.

For his nemesis Raymond Aron, it was precisely this simple-minded opposition of "humanity" to "power" that demonstrated the incapacity of French intellectuals since the Dreyfus Affair to understand the real challenges of twentieth-century European politics. In Aron's view, it was no accident, indeed it was utterly predictable, that Sartre's romantic ideal of commitment would turn him into a heartless apologist for Stalinism in the decade after World War II. In *L'Opium des intellectuels* (1955) Aron retold the story of the rise of the modern intellectual but with a decidedly antimythical intent, demonstrating how incompetent and naïve the intellectual as a class had been when it came to serious political matters. In his view, the real responsibility of European intellectuals after the war was to bring whatever expertise they had to bear on liberal-democratic politics and to maintain a sense of moral proportion in judging the relative injustices of different political systems—in short, to be independent spectators with a modest sense of their roles as citizens and opinion-makers. Sartre and his followers accepted no such responsibilities.

Aron was right: in France it was the romantic, "committed" intellectuals who served the cause of tyranny in the twentieth century.[18]

Thus if Aron intervenes in politics on the conservative side he is not irresponsible; but if Sartre does the same on the opposite side, he is utterly irresponsible. The same is true of Lilla's own politics. His telling us that we have to keep our mouths shut as George W. Bush wreaks havoc on the world is not irresponsibly political; but if we cry that our emperor's pants are on fire, we harbor reckless minds.

But why should Bush or Tony Blair be exempted from the same sort of critical inquiry we apply to Joseph Stalin and Saddam Hussein? An Iraqi journalist named Muntadar al-Zaidi threw his shoes at George W. Bush in Iraq as a protest against a war criminal, with the words "This is for the widows and orphans and all those killed in Iraq." Is he, too, a "reckless mind"—and how would Lilla deal with him? How can an intellectual be so blind to crimes against humanity? Is it because the perpetrators are white and the victims are colored and situated halfway around the globe?

The anti-intellectual catastrophe that Lilla exemplifies is not limited to right-wing professors and think-tankers. As Lilla rampages against any political engagement by public intellectuals, the very few of them who venture to lift voices of reason and sanity are left at the mercy of the empire's propaganda machinery. Today, even among the most perceptive voices in the United States, we discover that Islam and all its sacred, historical, and institutional referents have mutated into a metaphoric universe of terror and fanaticism. Thus Lewis H. Lapham, in his otherwise plangent critique of David Frum and Richard Perle's book *An End to Evil: How to Win the War on Terror* (which he rightly places among "the hundred-odd books made to the design specifications of a Pentagon press release"), falls into the trap of accepting the mutation of Islam from a world religion into an allegorical simulacrum of terror, backwardness, gibberish, and stupidity. He ridicules Frum and Perle for having borrowed their inspiration from "the verses of the Koran", for issuing "fatwas" like Osama bin Laden, and for summoning "all loyal and true Americans to the glory of jihad". He mocks them as "Mullah Frum","Mufti Perle", and "the two Washington ayatollahs", and he says, "Provide them with a beard, a turban, and a copy of the Koran, and I expect that they wouldn't have much trouble stoning to death a woman discovered in adultery with a cameraman from CBS News."[19]

If Lapham needs an appropriate metaphor to use for violence and unreason, can he not think of any other one than the Quran? Why can he not pause for a moment to think through the implications of his wording when he blasts Frum and Perle's book? He says:

> As with all forms of propaganda, the prose style doesn't warrant extensive quotation, but I don't do the authors a disservice by reducing their message to a series of divine commandments. Like Muhammad bringing the word of Allah to the widow Khadija and the well Zem-Zem, they aspire to a tone of voice appropriate to a book of Revelation.[20]

If Lapham needs an allegory to help with indoctrination in hatred and terror, why are Islam and Quranic language the first things that come to his mind?

> The result of their collaboration is an ugly harangue that if translated into Arabic and reconfigured with a few changes of word and emphasis (the objects of fear and loathing identified as America and Israel in place of Saudi Arabia and the United

Nations) might serve as a lesson taught to a class of eager jihadis at a madrasa in Kandahar.[21]

Far worse than the gibberish of a non-entity like Ibn Warraq is the lack of hesitation by one of the most acutely critical minds in the United States today in collapsing the entire sacred universe of a world religion—from its holy book to its prophet to its honorific titles—into a metaphor for stupidity, terrorism, banality, and fanaticism. One would have hoped for something finer in public discourse. But the propaganda machinery that generates and sustains its imperial imagery is so overwhelming that even critical thinkers like Lapham are not immune to it. Even those holding vigil against disastrous alliances with the ideologues of the New American Century have accepted a narrative constitution of evil, code-named Islam, that has dyed the very fabric of our public discourse with a self-fulfilling prophecy of doom and disaster.

THE TREASON OF THE INTELLECTUALS

This was the ideological atmosphere in which the figures of the comprador intellectual and the native informer suddenly emerged in force. The horror of the torture that occurred while Bush was driving the American military machinery also came to light in this atmosphere—and some key and crucial questions remained unanswered about this. According to a US Army report issued in August 2004 (known as the Fay Report), for example, at least 27 military intelligence personnel were guilty of torturing Iraqi prisoners at Abu Ghraib, near Baghdad. Senior commanders at the prison knew about the abuses but failed to act. (General Paul J. Kern, speaking on behalf of the committee that wrote the report, noted that the worst abuse occurred when dog handlers used their animals to try to make teenage detainees defecate out of fear.) The report found systematic torture of inmates "ranging from inhumane to sadistic". Meanwhile, as the *New York Times* reported, "classified parts of the report say Lt. Gen. Ricardo S. Sanchez approved the use in Iraq of some severe interrogation practices."[22]

Most of the public discussion that ensued focused on the responsibility of Secretary of Defense Donald Rumsfeld and officers at the Pentagon for the atrocities. And they were, of course, principally responsible. But a more thorough consideration must include the intellectual atmosphere of the moment. Public statements by a number of leading American legal and human-rights scholars and public intellectuals called, in fact, for legalizing torture. This idea gathered currency after the events of 9/11 and the revelation that the US had created an extra-territorial and extra-juridical concentration camp in the Guantanamo Bay detention facilities—where those designated "suspected terrorists" by the US government could be held indefinitely without charges or access to legal advice and, as "enemy combatants" denied even POW status, exempted from the mandates of the Geneva Conventions.

Shortly after the events of 9/11, Alan Dershowitz, the Felix Frankfurter Professor of Law at Harvard University, began campaigning for the legalization of torture—in newspaper articles, on television shows, and ultimately in a book. On November 8, 2001, for example, he argued for the viability of legalized torture in a *Los Angeles Times* article entitled, "Is There a Torturous Road to Justice?"[23] A year later, under another colorful title, "When All Else Fails, Why Not Torture", he made the same case in *American Legion Magazine*.[24] Shortly thereafter he made it again in a *60 Minutes* interview with Mike Wallace. He used the example of the "ticking bomb" to argue for torture as a legitimate way to prevent massive death tolls, and he added that because torture already existed it might as well be legalized: "If anybody has any doubt that our CIA, over time, has taught people to torture, has encouraged torture, has probably itself tortured in extreme cases, I have a bridge to sell you in Brooklyn."[25] In a subsequent interview with CNN's Wolf Blitzer, conducted before the revelations of Abu Ghraib, Dershowitz offered more specifics as to the forms of torture he would countenance: "I would talk about nonlethal torture, say, a sterilized needle underneath the nail, which would violate the Geneva Accords, but you know, countries all over the world violate the Geneva Accords."[26] In time he collected his thoughts into a definitive argument in his 2002 book *Why Terrorism Works*. (See Chapter Four: "Should the Ticking Bomb Terrorist Be Tortured? A Case Study in How a Democracy Should Make Tragic Choices."[27])

One might dismiss Dershowitz as a propagandist for the Jewish apartheid state, a committed Zionist, and argue that he is merely taking advantage of a frightened nation to score quick political points that support his world view. One might also argue that he is not really approaching this from an academic point of view, but rather, from a legal-technocratic angle. For a genuine intellectual discussion of torture we can turn to Michael Ignatieff—essayist, novelist, broadcaster, biographer of Isaiah Berlin, recipient of numerous literary prizes, former director of the Carr Center for

Human Rights Policy at Harvard University, and current leader of the Liberal Party in Canada: a major North American intellectual, widely read, deeply cultivated, and marvelously eloquent.

On the surface, Ignatieff seems to reject Dershowitz's call for legalized torture. But it takes him quite a few erudite pages in his book on the subject, *The Lesser Evil: Political Ethics in an Age of Terror* (2004), to say so—and these learned pages demand a very careful reading. Ignatieff says he believes that legalization of torture "is well-intentioned", but he is concerned that "as an exercise in the lesser evil it seems"—*seems!*—"likely to lead to the greater". He then adds emphatically, "Legalization of physical force in interrogation will hasten the process by which it becomes routine."[28] This is not exactly a rousing denunciation of torture, but it is nevertheless a qualified rejection of Dershowitz. If one were asked on the basis of this book whether Ignatieff is for or against legalizing torture, the answer would thus have to be in the negative, and in fact he states in the conclusion that "torture should remain anathema to a liberal democracy and should never be regulated, countenanced, or covertly accepted in a war on terror."[29]

But here, precisely, is the difference between a dangerous thesis lurking under learned and caring language and the bluster of a propagandist. Between Ignatieff's and Dershowitz's arguments, the lesser transgressor in the court of morals is Dershowitz's—his is only a distraction. Ignatieff's argument is infinitely worse. Without the slightest hesitation he calmly lays out all the legal, moral, ethical, and political ramifications of torture under certain extraordinary circumstances, weighing options, striking a balance here and a counterbalance there, and altogether appearing very judicious in his goal of saving a maximum number of lives under rather nasty circumstances—but, in effect, pursuing an agenda that lends justification to torture under certain circumstances.

The single acceptable response to the question of whether we should torture is no. Any other or lesser answer carries with it heinous implications that demand to be exposed—for here the intellectual has opted to serve the normative imaginary and stated objectives of his empire to the point of no return.

"There is no doubt about the moral facts," Ignatieff writes; "the question is whether democratic survival or national security could override the overwhelming claim that these facts usually make upon the allegiance of a liberal democracy."[30] It is a question he does not quite answer, but by raising it he has (cleverly) put it on the table—and thus suggested that one possible answer is yes, "democratic survival" and "national security" do override the moral prohibitions on torture. And with this move he has set in motion a discursive strategy of consistently providing excellent reasons for torture and then dismissing them with a sudden, single, perfunctory line. A crucial justification for torture followed by a shallow and empty rebuttal—thus he exploits all the fears and anxieties that the Bush administration sustained in the aftermath of 9/11.

Ignatieff thus operates on two simple and simultaneous narrative tracks: (1) providing the intellectual groundwork that eloquently and persuasively articulates why torture might sometimes be deemed necessary and (2) providing a cursory, vague defence of inalienable human rights. Consider the following example. First he posits the necessity of torture ("they" in the first line refers to "the terrorists"):

> The knowledge they possess may pose a mortal danger, if not to the survival of democratic society itself, then at least to large number of its citizens. Because this is so, many democracies nominally committed against torture have felt themselves compelled to torture in the name of necessity and national security.[31]

Then he proceeds to offer examples: France in Algeria, Israel in "the Occupied Territories" (as he calls Palestine), and the United States in Iraq. But first he dismisses the allegations of torture in Iraq (he wrote the book before the Abu Ghraib revelations) by noting that we do not have enough evidence; then he adds,

> given the uncertainties about the facts, it would seem essential for congress to insist on the right to tour detention facilities, to hold interviews with detainees in camera, and to disclose the information they get in closed session, so as to keep interrogation technique under democratic scrutiny.[32]

Compare the angry fist raised by "mortal danger", "survival of democratic society", "a large number of its citizens", and "national security" (all straight out of the post-9/11 propaganda machinery) with the pallid "it would seem essential for congress to insist on the right to tour detention facilities", "in camera," and "closed session". On one side we have a massive mobilization of Bush administration buzz words, on the other a limp attempt at reasonableness.

In a related move, Ignatieff first posits a logical inconsistency: "how can one object to the torture of persons to ensure valuable information for reasons of state, and not object to killing them?

Both could simply be regarded as acceptable lesser evils, forced on unwilling liberal democracies by the exigencies of their own survival."[33] And once again, the voice of fair-minded liberalism, he rejects his own suggestion—"the first takes a life; the second abuses one".[34] But in the process he has again planted an insidious seed and deepened the binary relation he consistently posits between "liberal democracies" (we, the civilized) and "terrorists" (they, the savages). In effect, he is telling readers: We are killing them anyway, so why can we not torture them, which not only is not as bad, they have forced us into it. (This used to be a rationalization of rapists: "She asked for it.")

"To save innocent civilians from imminent attack"[35] is the central leitmotif of Ignatieff's discussion. By "innocent civilians" he means Americans and Israelis. He fails to mention Iraqis, Afghans, Palestinians, Algerians, Arabs, and Muslims in general, and by extension any community that by resisting colonial occupation becomes "terrorist". Consider these sentences:

It might be argued that such dignity commitments [not to torture other people] are a luxury when a state is fighting for its life. But the Israeli case shows that a democratic state engaged in a war with terror can still maintain these commitments.[36]

Now, do not set foot on the immediate land mine and fall prey to anger at the identification of an apartheid, racist, supremacist, ethnocratic, fanatical, colonial settlement as "a democratic state"— that is a distraction. Concentrate instead on the even more insidious subtext of the proposition, which is (not so) hidden in the phrase "fighting for its life". Notice what that phrase does. It places a belligerent nation (either the imperial US or the colonial Israel) in a state of emergency under which it is forced to do things that under ordinary circumstances it would not wish to. So, if it tortures, assassinates, dispossesses, demolishes homes and livelihoods, forces populations into the indignity of exile and appropriates their land, it does so not out of its quintessential character but out of an incidental necessity—an accident rather than an essence as medieval philosophers used to put it. This humanist proposition puts the theorist in the superior position of making excruciating moral choices on behalf of two democratic states and thus ipso facto dehumanizes the object of its analysis—the Palestinian, the Iraqi, the Afghan, the Arab, the Muslim—every colored person who fails to grasp "the civilizing mission of the white man".

Ignatieff makes his case furtively, with a "there had been cases, in Israeli history, where physical methods of interrogation had actually saved lives"[37] here, an "if an interrogator violated the rules and engaged in torture, however, the [Israeli] court was prepared to accept necessity as a plea in mitigation, not as a justification or an excuse"[38] there. Euphemisms such as "physical methods of interrogation" gradually take the place of "torture". By now, Ignatieff's readers may be ready to accept his stipulation that the question is not simply torture but rather that "the problem lies in identifying the justifying exceptions and defining what forms of duress stop short of absolute degradation of an interrogation subject"—that is, how much, when, and where to twist arms, break bones, or pile prisoners naked on top of one another for a picture. Even now we must be careful not to be derailed by this obscenity, because the real atrocity lies in the phrase "an interrogation subject": the prisoner has ceased to be a person with a name, a family, convictions, politics, humanity. He or she is nothing but "an interrogation subject" ready to be tortured at Abu Ghraib or some nameless Israeli site.

But Ignatieff does not stop at dehumanizing the tortured; he must also reassert the primary humanity of the torturer. "A further problem with physical torture," he stipulates "is that it inflicts damage on those who perpetrate it as well as those who are forced to endure it." More specifically, "Torture exposes agents of a democratic state to ultimate moral hazard."[39] The point is that since the torturers belong to the humanity of the "democratic states", they can ultimately pose a threat to "the health of their own societies". While one could argue that torture also damages the torturer, it is perverse, to say the least, to imply any equivalence between the damage inflicted on the torturer and the tortured. He gives too much significance to any hazard there might be to the health and humanity of his fellow citizens in the US and Israel.

One may deduce (or hope) that the phrase "as well as those who are forced to endure it" at least acknowledges the humanity of the tortured. But such is not the case. The principal problem with torture is not the violation of the victim's humanity but, Ignatieff writes, that "those who are subjected to physical torture, when not actually broken psychologically, usually conceive undying hatred for their torturer."[40] Now we have a problem on our hands—but Ignatieff, as usual, has a handy solution. "One way around this problem, obviously, is to dispose of the tortured, in order to prevent their returning as a threat."[41] How more meticulously premeditated could a criminal act be? To be sure, Ignatieff then insists that the "democratic state" should have nothing to do with such a final solution, because "once torture becomes a state practice, it entrains further consequences that can poison the moral reputation and political legitimacy of a state."[42] But he puts the proposition on the table anyway, while attributing it to such "non-democratic" states as Chile and Argentina in past decades. He fails to mention that CIA agents—"agents of a democratic state", as he calls them— were directly involved in the atrocities in Chile and Argentina (and any number of other strategic countries around the world, including Iran).

It is not enough for Ignatieff to dehumanize the victims of torture (at the very moment when American guards were perpetrating their crimes against humanity at Abu Ghraib). It is not even enough for him to cast them as criminals to begin with who become even more murderous after being tortured. He must go further. Since he finds a "moral hazard" in the act of torture "for everyone involved",[43] he proposes that "it is worth listening to the testimony of one of torture's victims".[44] At this point in a book about the systematic dehumanization of populations who say no to the imperial hubris of a criminal attempt at empire building, you might reasonably expect to hear the voice of one of them: an Afghan, a Palestinian, an Iraqi—an Arab, a Muslim. Yet again you would be wrong in such an assumption.

The only example that Ignatieff can come up with is "Jean Amery, a Belgian resistant" who was "arrested in Brussels in 1943 for distributing tracts in German urging soldiers of the German occupation to desert. He was tortured by the SS in a Belgian jail in 1943, before being shipped off to Auschwitz".[45] Not an Arab, not a Muslim, not one of the current victims of torture that Ignatieff has dehumanized with George W. Bush and his cabal by labeling them "terrorists". To have a Palestinian tell what it means to be tortured by Israelis in Tel Aviv, or an Iraqi by Americans in Abu Ghraib, or an Afghan by Americans in Kandahar would risk giving them back an iota of their humanity. The small dignity he might restore to thousands of tortured Palestinians, Iraqis, and Afghans at the threshold of the twenty-first century he awards to a Belgian in 1943. The European becomes the voice of the tortured body. Now, if you allow yourself to become angry at and get distracted by Ignatieff's use of the loaded name "Auschwitz" to drum up the memory of the Nazi atrocities and thus lend legitimacy to the Zionist colonial settlement in Palestine, you may miss the far more serious crime he has perpetrated by robbing millions of people around the world of their humanity.

Having systematically dehumanized the whole of humanity, minus those with the honor of living in such liberal democracies as the United States and Israel, Ignatieff identifies Iraq, Burma, and North Korea (his slight variation on George Bush's Iraq-Iran-North Korea "Axis of Evil") as representative of the rest: "For these societies, the practice of torture is definitional of their very identity as forms of state power. This idea helps us to see why torture should remain anathema to a liberal democracy and should never be regulated, countenanced, or covertly accepted in a war on terror."[46] Having just laid out, in detail, exactly the opposite of this bravura conclusion on torture by demonstrating how liberal democracies—"alas"—have to perpetrate it, the finale brings his argument to the level of a manifest destiny and the civilizing mission mandated as the white man's burden. "Definitional" to these societies—that is, the portion of humanity not blessed to live in Israel and the United States—is the practice of torture, which is what the United States and Israel must face, and this, Ignatieff believes, is no new challenge to the white man. "Terrorism does not present us with a distinctively new temptation. This is what our institutions were designed for, back in the seventeenth century: to regulate evil means and control evil people."[47] The Arabs and Muslims resisting colonial domination of their homeland today thus find themselves placed next to millions of native Americans and African slaves as "evil people" with the "evil means" to disrupt the white man's civilizing mission and destroy his plantations.

As we have seen, if you are careful, it is possible to avoid all the booby traps that Michael Ignatieff has planted, catch him at his game, and force him to expose his hand. Now, let us plant him a few booby traps of our own.

Suppose that on the evening of July 1, 1946, the British authorities had captured a certain Menachem Begin (the future Prime Minister of Israel), whom they had solid reason to believe was the leader of a terrorist organization called Irgun, and who was about to blow up the King David Hotel in Jerusalem and kill scores of innocent civilians. Suppose that on the evening of April 9, 1948, the Palestinian residents of Deir Yassin had captured a certain Yitzhak Shamir (another future Prime Minister of Israel) and were led to believe he was in possession of vital information about a pending massacre of the residents of their village. Suppose, alternatively, that in December 1947 Palestinians had captured both

Begin and Shamir with solid information about pending attacks on Palestinian civilians in villages near Haifa and in Safad, Tabaraya, al-Tireh, Saasa, Kfar Husseiniya, Sarafand, Kalounya, Beyt Sourik, Aylaboun, al-Shajara, and Nasser Al-Dine that would place the lives of thousands of Palestinian men, women, and children in imminent danger. Suppose that in February 1942 the Turkish authorities had just captured Zionist terrorists who were about to blow up the ship Stroma carrying 770 illegal Jewish emigrants. Suppose that, in 1948, the Iraqi authorities had captured members of Zionist terrorist organizations who were about to implement the operations they called Ali Baba and Magic Carpet to blow up Jewish residential areas in Baghdad in order to force the Iraqi Jews to move to Israel. Just to play the devil's advocate, suppose also that in autumn 1956 the Palestinian residents of Kfar Kassem and Khan Younis had captured a member of the Hagana terrorist organizations that they had been led to believe was about to wipe out Palestinian civilians. Suppose that in the early morning hours of October 14, 1953, the Palestinian residents of the village of Qibya had captured a certain Ariel Sharon (another future Prime Minister of Israel) and were almost sure he was about to lead his squad on a mission to blow up their houses and murder their families. Suppose that one fine April day in 1973 Lebanese authorities captured a suspicious-looking woman and her companion, took them to police station in Ras Beirut, and discovered that she was actually a man in disguise—a certain Ehud Barak (another future Prime Minister of Israel)—and that he was about to assassinate a number of Palestinian leaders. The list can go on ad nauseum.

But just for good measure, imagine finally that on the evening of September 16, 1982, members of the PLO had yet again captured Ariel Sharon and knew that he was about to unleash the savage Lebanese Phalangists on the two camps of Sabra and Shatila in Beirut, where they would slaughter hundreds of Palestinian refugees. Now then: under these circumstances, would Michael Ignatieff consider the possibility of torturing Menachem Begin, Yitzhak Shamir, Ehud Barak, and Ariel Sharon and all their terrorist accomplices in what he calls "the liberal democracy" of the Jewish state of Israel in order to extract information from them about these particular ticking bombs?

If the renowned terrorists of yesterday are the recent and current leaders of a "liberal democracy", then what is the difference between them and the man who once said, "After all, who today speaks of the extermination of the Armenians?"

VENAL, VAGABOND, ROOTLESS, AND MERCENARY

To understand the political climate and the social conditions in which the *comprador intellectuals* in general and the *native informers* in particular fermented and emerged in the United States of the neo-conservative era, it is imperative not to be limited by the notion of *exilic intellectuals* as Edward Said understood it, which is effectively a sword and can cut both ways—for every Said there are at least ten Fouad Ajamis. Nor is it sufficient to map out the panoply of rogue American leadership, from George W. Bush on down. We must add a militant cell of neoconservative Zionists (now active, now sleeping)—Irving Kristol, William Kristol, Norman Podhoretz, and their ilk—to the picture, along with such prominent theoreticians as Francis Fukuyama and Samuel Huntington and their kindred spirits Mark Lilla, Alan Dershowitz, and Michael Ignatieff. All this gives us a clearer conception of the calamity that has conditioned the rise of the malady we call *native informers*, and it all points to a more fundamental malady in the American social condition—historically known as *the politics of mass society*—that makes it chronically susceptible to intellectual charlatanism.

In his study of the relationship of various social classes to mass societies, *The Politics of Mass Society* (1959), William Kornhauser examined the function of what he called "unattached intellectuals" in facilitating a frenzied atmosphere of fear and domination that is conducive to atomization of individuals—citizens of a republic cut off from the "web of group affiliation",[48] as the German sociologist Georg Simmel put it, and thus susceptible to populist and fascist movements. Separated from their organic links to their class, community, and nation, these unattached intellectuals "create millennial appeals in response to their own sense of the loss of social function and relatedness in the mass society".[49] Over them hovers an atmosphere of anomie, isolation, disconnectedness, anxiety, and rootlessness. "Free-lance intellectuals," Kornhauser observes, "appear to be more disposed toward mass movements than intellectuals in corporate bodies (especially universities)."[50] He then summarizes:

> Five reasons may be advanced for the hypothesis that free-lance intellectuals are more receptive to political extremism than are

other types of intellectuals. First, the free-lance intellectual ... has been dependent on an anonymous and unpredictable market. He has had to start his enterprise anew every generation, and as a result is in an anxiety-arousing position similar to that of the first-generation small businessman. Much more rooted and culturally integrated are those intellectuals who enter into old and stable organizations, such as universities. Second, free-lance intellectuals tend to have fewer institutional responsibilities than intellectuals in professional organizations, and therefore are less likely to be committed to central institutions. Third, rewards are much less certain to be forthcoming for the free-lance intellectual, the form of reward less predictable, and the permanence of the recognition more tenuous ... Fourth, free-lance intellectuals ... tend to be more dependent on their audience, over which they have relatively little control, and to feel greater social distance from it, in contrast to, for example, the professor in relation to his students. Fifth, free-lance intellectuals suffer more when there is an over-supply of intellectuals. In general, a condition of chronic overcrowding of the professions engenders large numbers of discontented and alienated intellectuals of all kinds. This was the situation in Germany following World War I.[51]

It is remarkable to see how applicable Kornhauser's observations, made in 1950s Germany in the aftermath of the Nazi era, are to the United States in the neoconservative era. A common thread links Lewis, Ajami, Nafisi, Hirsi Ali, Rushdie, Warraq, and scores of others like them as comprador intellectuals. They are all (1) immigrant; (2) either scholars or academics; and (3) intellectuals with close connections to the US centers of power, and the military establishment in particular.

Equally important in understanding comprador intellectuals are the insights of Theodor Geiger, who as early as 1949 (and also on the basis of his observations in Nazi Germany), declared:

Those less qualified aspirants for practical-academic positions, especially those who have not even succeeded in passing their exams, will attempt to make their way as "free intelligentsia". Journalism was (and in part still is) a preferred refuge for such types ... To fill the demands of a practical-academic profession, a specified and measurable amount of knowledge is required. The entrance into the free intelligentsia is not subject to such a control. There are no exams or minimum qualifications.[52]

Kornhauser's insights now need updating to encompass our more advanced stage of a globally atomized planet over which a predatory capitalism wishes to preside. Moreover, we cannot share his rather too sanguine optimism about the tenured professoriate's innate resistance to the danger of incorporation into the class of rootless or what he calls "unattached" intellectuals. Though both he and Geiger are correct in their observation that scholars who have not succeeded in establishing reputable academic credentials are much more likely to become mercenary intellectuals at the whim of the politics and commerce of the free-market economy, he disregards a danger of a different sort that threatens the tenured professoriate. This latter category is obviously more susceptible to the internal politics of universities, not to mention the external politics of grants and fellowships from both private and governmental sources.[53] While their institutional affiliations, the review processes integral to universities, and their tenure all help to protect them against the political and commercial whims of the free market, the very same forces are likely to produce minds that, if they do not exactly serve power, systematically accommodate it.

For this reason, the question of academic freedom is something of a red herring. The more fundamental question is intellectual freedom, which is a public concern not limited to the private sphere of the university. Those very few academic intellectuals who venture out of their classrooms and speak openly and courageously on public issues are, in fact, the exceptions that prove the rule that academic privatization has made them not so much complacent as indifferent to power—because by the time they receive their tenure, bending backward to accommodate power has become second nature to them.

The home-grown comprador intellectuals and the native informers imported from the farthest corners of the empire, white or whitewashed, have joined forces with capital, very much like the mercenary armies that the empire recruits to fight its wars; it is no accident that both Ajami and Nafisi have worked for Paul Wolfowitz or that Seyyed Vali Reza Nasr and Ray Takeyh have taught at US military colleges. The task of the globalized comprador intellectual is quite clear. The empire needs to destroy all communities and cultures that may be the potential sites of resistance to what Max Weber called "predatory capitalism" and its corresponding planetary (homogenized) culture. The labor is divided between immigrant intellectuals (Ajami, Nafisi, Rushdie, Lewis) and comprador intellectuals native to the empire. But this division of labor disappears in the larger context of an economic and cultural globalization contingent on an amorphous, decentered capitalism and the disappearance of communal, national, and regional cultures, convictions, and principles. The imperial machinery has put them all to work and made them homeless thinkers, the intellectual arm of Blackwater USA.

The current conception of the "terrorist" tends to be a stateless, homeless, cultureless, violent entity set to destroy the "civilized" world—i.e. the United States and Israel. And that is precisely the image of the comprador intellectual, and above all the native informer, that has emerged to combat this "terrorist"—equally stateless, homeless, characterless and cultureless, a "citizen of a portable world".

EMPIRES DO NOT LAST

If empires were permanent, everyone would be speaking Persian now, and I would be writing in my mother tongue. I write, instead, in the mother tongue of somebody else whose ancestors had guns more powerful than Cyrus the Great could ever have imagined. Thus (fortunately) I had to learn another imperial language.

In the remnants of the Persian imperial imagination, however, we have a medieval text, *Chahar Maqaleh-ye Aruzi*, in which a chapter is devoted to poets and their necessity to the smooth operation of a kingdom—or an empire.[54] They sing the praises of the emperor in beautiful and memorable words, which are memorized by the courtiers and through them handed along to the rest of the world. It is not so much that people are ignorant of the emperor's atrocities as that they have fallen prey to the beauty of the poet's lies.

There is a popular twist to this notion in a story told about a court poet who was exceptionally talentless in invention but who had a prodigious gift for memorization. He had to hear a poem only once to know it by heart. His wife had an almost equally amazing memory, but she had to hear the poem twice. Their son had inherited his parents' gift, but he had to hear a poem thrice to remember it. And the household's nearly-as-talented servant had to hear it four times. The entrepreneurial consequence of these four prodigious memories was that whenever a poet came to the court to recite a new poem for the king, the court poet would call him a liar and a plagiarist, and to prove that even the lengthiest poem was his own he would proceed to recite it from beginning to end. Then he would add, "Your Majesty, my wife knows it, too"—and, having now heard it twice, she would recite it, too. Then would follow the son and the servant.

For years, the story goes, no poet in the land could win glory at this notorious court because his poem would be stolen on the spot by this bandit family. Finally, one day a wily poet appeared and declared that he had a new poem for the king. The court gathered, and the new arrival began reciting his poem. Two lines into it he stopped, turned to the court poet, and said, "If this poem is yours, then finish it." Thus was the court poet's charlatanism exposed.

The moral of the story is that even if you can fool everyone once and you can probably fool an emperor all the time, you cannot, in Abraham Lincoln's words, fool all of the people all of the time. The difference between Said's exilic intellectual and the comprador intellectual who has treacherously lurked in the shadow of that very defiant voice is the difference between those two proverbial poets. While they both recite at the court of the emperor, one of them serves his master by consistently repeating a lie, while the other subverts and disrupts that lie by commencing a poem that his rival can neither conceive nor complete. I will leave it to Michael Ignatieff to find out how this particular parable will end. Then he can tell Alan Dershowitz.

3
Literature and Empire

Me, a Negress? Can't you see I'm almost white. I hate niggers. Niggers stink. They're dirty and lazy. Don't ever mention niggers to me.

> A Woman from Martinique, as quoted by
> Fanon in *Black Skins, White Masks* (1952)

There is a fundamental difference between the manifestations of anti-Muslim racism in Europe and in the United States—and this difference makes the market for the native informer's services doubly profitable in the latter. While, in Europe, classical anti-Semitism is now being transfigured into assaults on the rights of Muslim citizens, in the United States such rights as wearing a scarf or attending a religious school have seldom been questioned.[1] In Europe, Islamophobia is largely manifested in the antagonism of most European Union (EU) states toward Turkish membership, and in their condescending attitude toward indigenous Muslim communities in the former Yugoslavia and other Eastern European enclaves, and multiplied by the denial of full citizenship rights to new Muslim émigrés in countries like Germany, France, and Austria. (Turkey was officially recognized as a candidate for full membership of the European economic and political union in 1999, but full accession is unlikely to happen until at least 2013. Turkey must fulfill the requirements of EU law and then member states must unanimously agree on its entry.) It is here, in the attempt to sustain a white racist conception of Europe, that the services of native informers come in handy.

In the United States, where the situation is quite different, the services that native informers find most profitable have to do with the wars against Muslim countries that George W. Bush's presidency in particular created and sustained. Thus, where the European market for native informers is prolonged, steady, and *longue durée*, the American one is unpredictable, volatile, and, precisely for these reasons, more lucrative. The European market yields the native informer a steady but relatively low income, while the American one offers a short-term but quite handsome windfall. If Rushdie's position on the Muhammad cartoon row typifies the services that native informers can lend the European market to demonize Islam and intimidate Muslim communities into submission to the whim and will of white racists, Azar Nafisi's publication of *Reading Lolita in Tehran* in 2003, shortly before the invasion of Iraq, performs the same function in the American context. We now need to take a closer look at just how Nafisi was reading *Lolita* in Tehran.

HEGEMONY AND EMPIRE

During the final round of the 2004 US presidential contest between President George W. Bush and Senator John Kerry, at one point the public debate over their differences came down to competing notions of *an empire with no hegemony* (for Bush) versus a *hegemony with no empire* (for Kerry). The issue remained unresolved, but with the re-election of Bush for a second term the question of whether the empire that he was now leading possessed or lacked a dominant ideology persisted. Did he and his vociferous band of neoconservative ideologues have an imperial design for the world based on a hegemonic set of dominant discourses—or did they simply wish to rule with an iron fist, rather than cultivating consent via the velvet glove of a legitimacy?

In mid-April 2006, the veteran investigative reporter Seymour Hersh published an article in *The New Yorker* exposing an apparent Pentagon plan to attack Iran[2] that marked the first time since Hiroshima and Nagasaki that the use of nuclear weaponry had been seriously contemplated. Anti-war activists all over the world were alerted to this frightful extension of US militarism; an organization of scientists issued a warning, in the form of a video simulation, that such a tactical use of a nuclear weapon would mean the immediate deaths of at least three million people and expose millions more to cancer-causing agents, with the domain of the catastrophe extending eastward into Afghanistan, Pakistan, and even India.

Conspicuously absent from the public response was any awareness that the Bush administration's rhetoric against Iran was all but identical with what it had brought to bear only a few years earlier against Afghanistan and Iraq. Such cookie-cutter phrases as "war on terror", "Islamic terrorism", and "promoting democracy", were repeated *ad nauseum* in what appeared to be historical amnesia, with Iran's president, Mahmoud Ahmadinejad, standing where Osama bin Laden and Saddam Hussein had stood earlier. The American media and the public at large treated this threat of war on Iran as if they had not heard the identical phrases just a few years earlier. Not only CNN, the *New York Times*, Fox News, and the usual New York-based Zionist tabloids, but even segments of the anti-war movement failed to connect the dots.

This collective amnesia in a period during which the catastrophic consequences of the invasions of Afghanistan and Iraq were yet to be fully assayed once again raised the question of hegemony and empire. Was there a method to the madness of US military adventurism around the globe? Did this empire have a hegemonic project, or an ideological agenda to justify its global warmongering? Or, was it merely making a mess around the world without moral or political accountability for the terror it was perpetrating?

To be sure, historians have sought to theorize the historical domains of the emerging US empire. Niall Ferguson, in *Colossus: The Price of American Empire* (2004), has called the American empire "the imperialism of anti-imperialism"—that is, a form of global domination that does not like to be called by its real name and that in fact posits itself as a liberating force.[3] On the other side of the spectrum, Michael Hardt and Antonio Negri had, even before the cataclysmic events of 9/11, articulated a theoretical position in *Empire* (2000), arguing that classical imperialism had now mutated into an imperial mode of domination corresponding to cultural, social, and economic globalization but, in fact, rooted in American constitutionalism.[4] The pre-eminent historian Eric Hobsbawm, in a new (2005) preface to V. G. Kiernan's *America, The New Imperialism: From White Settlement to World Hegemony* (1978), argued that so far as Anglo-American imperialists were concerned, "the rest of humanity was only a raw material, clay to be molded by the potter's hand. This assumption of superiority may be called a legacy of British insularity, magnified by America's size and wealth."[5] Meanwhile, the American Chalmers Johnson, in his magnificent *The Sorrows of Empire: Militarism, Secrecy, and the End of Republic* (2004), was providing a thoroughly documented yet mournful eulogy to the demise of the American republic, from whose ashes a predatory empire was rising.[6] Other observers, like Michael Mann in *Incoherent Empire* (2003) and Robert D. Kaplan in *Imperial Grunts: The American Military on the Ground* (2005), address both the theory and the facts of the militarist dominions of this empire.[7]

COLLECTIVE AMNESIA, SELECTIVE MEMORY

As part of this more general interest in American empire, one might also point out that the way the US propaganda machinery has operated since 9/11, both domestically and globally, is also contingent on collective amnesia—a nefarious reliance on the presumption that no one is watching, no one is counting, and no one is keeping a record of anything; that memory and history are both dead. This proposition tallies well with the principal thesis that set this predatory new phase of empire in motion, namely Francis Fukuyama's notion of "the end of history", which in this context amounts to the effective erasure of even the most recent shared experiences, which must coalesce to prompt meaningful social action if not political movements.

How could one account for this politically expedited collective amnesia, by which consent is manufactured and history is discarded at the speed of one major military operation every couple of years? One way of decoding the trauma that followed 9/11 is to read it as a form of historical amnesia in response to the global spectacle in which the seemingly invulnerable was revealed as vulnerable. The trauma of 9/11 was far worse than that of Pearl Harbor, with which it is usually compared, because of the sheer magnitude of the visual spectacle. The Armageddon-like crumbling of the twin towers showed the vulnerability of globalized capital's totem poles, symbols of its monumental potency. That vulnerability was too disturbing to be allowed to be remembered. As globalized capital is amorphous, so did its enemy become faceless—a mere band of anonymous terrorists who came from nowhere and ended up dead, with their bodies dissolved in the ashes of the towers they had brought down. The faceless enemy did, however, need to have a momentary face and a location, for the erasure of collective memory required the fabrication of a short-term memory that in its intensity over-compensated for the shortness of its duration. The more fiercely Osama Bin Laden, al-Qaeda, the Taliban, and Afghanistan were depicted as principal targets of the War on Terror, the shorter the historical memory necessary to sustain the delusion. Two years after Bin Laden and Afghanistan came Saddam Hussein and Iraq, and after another two years Ahmadinejad and Iran. Fabricating successive enemies thus became the principal *modus operandi* of the empire: one to two wars per presidential election.

One may also argue that this act of collective amnesia accompanies a strategy of selective memory to cover its own traces. A particularly powerful example is now fully evident in an increasing body of Muslim women's memoirs that has, over the past half-decade, ever since the commencement of the War on Terror, flooded the US market. This body of literature, perhaps best represented by

Reading Lolita in Tehran, points to legitimate concerns about the plight of Muslim women in the Islamic world and yet puts that predicament squarely at the service of American warmongering. "Islam" in this particular reading is vile, violent, and above all abusive of women—and thus to fight against Islamic terrorism is to save Muslim women from their own men—"white men saving brown women from brown men," as the distinguished postcolonial theorist Gayatri Chakravorty Spivak puts it in her seminal essay, "Can the Subaltern Speak?"[8]

HOME IN THE HEART OF AN EMPIRE

Some years after the publication of *Reading Lolita in Tehran* in 2003, faced with continuing concern about yet another American military operation in the region, one can now clearly see how very effectively the book cultivated US (and by extension global) public opinion against Iran, after it had already provided a key propaganda tool to the Bush administration during its prolonged wars in Afghanistan and Iraq. A closer examination of the text reveals much about the way the US imperial design operates in Islamic domains.

With one strike, Nafisi achieved three perfidious outcomes: (1) the systematic denigration of an entire culture of revolutionary resistance to a history of colonialism; (2) the advancement of the cultural foregrounding of a predatory empire; and (3) a catering to the most reactionary forces within the United States as they waged a war against immigrant communities seeking curricular recognition on university campuses.

Not since Betty Mahmoody's notorious *Not Without My Daughter* (1984)[9] has a text exuded so visceral a hatred of everything Iranian, from the country's people to its literary masterpieces. By offering a Kaffeeklatsch version of English literature as the ideological foregrounding of American empire, *Reading Lolita in Tehran* is reminiscent of the most pestiferous colonial projects of the British in India; it brings to mind the words of Thomas Macaulay, who as a colonial officer in 1835, decreed, "We must do our best to form a class who may be interpreters between us and the millions whom we govern, a class of persons Indian in blood and colour, but English in taste, in opinions, words and intellect."[10] Within the United States, *Reading Lolita in Tehran* vigorously promoted the cause of Western literature at a moment when multicultural scholars and activists on university campuses had finally succeeded in introducing a modicum of curricular attention to world literatures. To achieve all of this while employed by US Deputy Secretary of Defense Paul Wolfowitz, indoctrinated by the father of American neoconserva-tives, Leo Strauss (and his infamous tract Persecution and the Art of Writing),[11] coached by the Lebanese Shi'i neocon artist Fouad Ajami, wholeheartedly endorsed by Bernard Lewis, and celebrated by an entire platoon of US old-school conservatives and neocons (from George Will to Christopher Hitchens) is quite a feat for a little-known professor of English literature at an Iranian university without a single previous credible book or scholarly credential to her name.

Nafisi's book is the locus classicus of the ideological foregrounding of imperial domination in three ways. (1) It banks on the collective amnesia toward American moves for global domination, beginning with its failure to thwart the Iranian revolution of 1979 and continuing with the catastrophic aftermath of the invasion of Iraq—for in *Reading Lolita in Tehran* there is a conspicuous absence of the historical and a blatant whitewashing of the literary; (2) It exemplifies the abuse of legitimate causes (in this case women's repression) for illegitimate purposes (US global domination); (3) Through the instrumentality of English literature, recycled and articulated by an Oriental woman who deliberately casts herself as a contemporary Scheherazade, it seeks to provoke the darkest corners of Euro-American Oriental fantasies and thus neutralize competing sites of cultural resistance to US imperial designs both at home and abroad. Only on the surface is *Reading Lolita in Tehran* limited to denigrating Iranian, and by extension, Islamic literary cultures; its equally important effect is to denigrate competing non-white immigrant cultures, from African to Asian to Latin American, and other racial minorities.

PLOTTING THE ENEMY

Reading Lolita in Tehran has a simple plot. The narrator, a professor of English literature at an Iranian university, born to a privileged family and thus educated in Europe and the United States, grows fed up with the limitations on life in the Islamic Republic. She resigns her post and collects together seven of the brightest women, gathering them at her home to read a few masterpieces of "Western literature"; and she connects the characters and incidents in the novels they read to their own daily difficulties. This plot, whether factual or manufactured or some combination of the two, provides the occasion for a sweeping condemnation of not only the Islamic revolution but also the nation that gave rise to it.

To understand how this simple plot extends its services to US imperial operations in the region, we need a larger theoretical frame of reference—which Edward Said has provided in his magisterial 1993 study of the cultural foregrounding of imperialism, *Culture and Imperialism*. In this book Said examined the overlapping territories, as he called them, of the literary and the political, the cultural and the imperial, in the Euro-American imperial imaginary.[12] His project, as he never tired of repeating, was not to reduce European literature to its political proclivities but rather to posit politics as the principal interlocutor of the literary event.

In *The Anarchy of Empire in the Making of US Culture* (2002), Amy Kaplan has demonstrated the link between domestic and foreign affairs in the manufacturing of such an imperial project.[13] In this groundbreaking literary investigation, Kaplan shows how at least since the middle of the nineteenth century and the commencement of successive wars with Mexico, Spain, Cuba and the Philippines, American imperial expansionism has been tightly bound with domestic political issues, especially race, class, and gender.

From the other side of the same argument, in her equally extraordinary *Masks of Conquest: Literary Study and British Rule in India* (1989), Gauri Viswanathan has shown how the study of English literature became an effective strategy of colonial control,[14] facilitating British rule via the education of a generation of Indians who, as Macaulay put it, were "Indian in blood and colour, but English in taste, in opinions, words and intellect."

In Said, Kaplan, and Viswanathan we have a body of scholarship that puts forward a persuasive argument as to how the teaching of literature has historically been definitive of British—and now American—imperial proclivities. Again, none of these scholars reduces the literary event to the political fact; rather, they posit a political interlocutor next to the work of literature. One can similarly offer a feminist or an anti-racist critique of the same texts without compromising their literary significance.

Reading Lolita in Tehran is the most cogent contemporary case of positing English literature as a means of manufacturing trans-regional cultural consent to Euro-American domination. Nafisi's connection to leading neoconservatives and her systematic denigration of Iranian culture are additional (though not essential) factors (1) placing her squarely at the service of US imperialism and (2) making her a partner in this project—for which plotting the domain of *the enemy*, in a classically Schmittian manner, outside the normative and moral purview of English language, literature, and culture is the *conditio sine qua non*.

DE-NARRATING A NATION

The transmutation of Nafisi from a legitimate critic of the Islamic Republic into an ideologue for George W. Bush's empire-building project provides a crucial lesson in the way the new breed of comprador intellectuals and native informers[15] is being recruited and put to use in the ideological build-up (and the cultural foregrounding) of an otherwise precarious claim to imperial hegemony. Her case merits attention far beyond the ordinary banalities of career opportunists. The critical task is to perceive the manner in which comprador intellectuals sustain an impoverished imperial imagination that seeks to pacify, eliminate, or neutralize cultures of resistance to it. Camouflaged as critics of the tyranny that has brutalized postcolonial nations, comprador intellectuals generate and sustain a level of public sentiment that discredits those nations at the very core of their resistance to the emerging empire. A principal effect of *Reading Lolita in Tehran* is to discredit a national culture—its pride of place, its will to resist both domestic and foreign tyranny, and ultimately the normative predicates of its own location in history.

By definition, comprador intellectuals must be able to feign cultural authenticity. Nafisi was an assistant professor of literature who suffered the abuses that the ideological machinery of the Islamic Republic has perpetrated on secular intellectuals. When she felt her career was being compromised, she had the financial resources to resign—a privilege available to few other Iranian faculty members suffering under a beleaguered theocracy whose fanaticism is exacerbated by ongoing threats from an equally fanatical Christian empire and Jewish state. Nafisi left Iran rightfully indignant and found in the United States new opportunities opening up within the Oriental regiment of the neocons (with Dinesh D'Souza and Fouad Ajami now attracting younger talents to their ranks). Nafisi arrived jobless in 1997 but soon published an essay in *The New Republic* showing off her talents, which was when Paul Wolfowitz and Fouad Ajami offered her an adjunct position at Johns Hopkins University.

In the immediate aftermath of 9/11, comprador intellectuals were actively sought out by the militant ideologues of the US Empire. Their task was to feign authority, authenticity, and native knowledge by informing the American public of the atrocities taking place in the region of their birth, thereby justifying the imperial designs of the United States as a liberation. Nafisi's book appeared precisely at a time when President George W. Bush had initiated his planetary imperial project by launching a global War on Terror and grouped Iran, Iraq, and North Korea together as an Axis of Evil. As in so many instances of propaganda and disinformation, *Reading Lolita in Tehran* is predicated on an element of truth. The Islamic Republic of Iran has an atrocious record of stifling, silencing, and murdering oppositional intellectuals. But the function of the comprador intellectual is less to expose such atrocities than to package them in a manner that best serves the empire they help to sustain. Under the guise of legitimate criticism they effectively perpetuate (indeed aggravate) the domestic terror they purport to expose. Plotting the enemy in a narrative of demonization and de-narrating a nation from its historical claim to authority both pave the way for the advance of the colonial combat battalion.

AN ICONIC BURGLARY

Because comprador intellectuals (true to the origin of the term *comprador* as a facilitator of commercial transactions) operate within the middle-class morality of their host country (now mutated into an empire), innuendo and insinuation are among their principal tools. By far the most immediately intriguing aspect of *Reading Lolita in Tehran* is its cover, which shows two young Iranian women with heads bent forward in an obvious posture of reading. What exactly is it they are reading we do not see or know. Above them we first read *Reading Lolita* and then, on a second line, *in Tehran*, and below we have the picture of the two teenagers. The immediate suggestion is very simple. The subject of the book is reading Vladimir Nabokov's *Lolita* in the city of Tehran, and here are two Iranian-looking teenagers in headscarves reading (something or other). They appear happily engaged, so endearing that they solicit sympathy, even complicity. What better picture to represent the idea of reading *Lolita* in Tehran than two teenage girls reading (something or other)? The imagination of the observer fills in what they are reading: Vladimir Nabokov's novel *Lolita*. Right? Wrong.

A moment of pause over this cover begins to reveal something more pernicious. The image and the caption together—in an example of the classical instance analyzed by Roland Barthes in his magnificent essay "The Photographic Message"—suggest the tantalizing addition of an Oriental. Both as social sign and as literary signifier, the term "Lolita" invokes illicit sex with teenagers, the obsessive indulgence of an old man with a young girl. Then, the fact that these two teenage faces are framed by headscarves suggestively borrows and insidiously unleashes an Oriental fantasy and binds it to the most lurid case of pedophilia in the modern literary imagination. Under the rubric of *photographic paradox*, Barthes offered a brilliant diagnosis of the way an imitative art like photography "comprises two messages: a *denoted* message, which is the *analogon* itself, and a *connoted* message, which is the matter in which the society to a certain extent communicates what it thinks of it."[16]

The *denoted* message here seems quite obvious: These two young women are reading *Lolita* in Tehran. They are reading the novel *Lolita* and they are in Tehran (they look Iranian and they have on headscarves). The *connoted* message is equally obvious: Imagine— illicit sex with teenagers in the Islamic Republic! How about that! the cover proposes suggestively. Can you imagine reading *Lolita* in *Tehran*? Look at these two Oriental Lolitas! The racist implication of the suggestion—also implicit in the astonishment of asking, "Can you even imagine reading that novel in that country?"—competes with the Orientalized pedophilia and confounds the barefaced transparency of a marketing strategy that appeals to the most deranged Oriental fantasies of a nation already scared out of its wits by a ferocious war against a phantasmagoric Arab/Muslim male potency that has just castrated the two totemic phalluses of the American empire.

The image of the two girls from the mysteriously veiled Orient is a dose straight out of Bernard Lewis's medicine cabinet: the erotic infantilization of the Orient. One of the most common clichés of Oriental desire is the under-aged man and woman, staged in innumerable Orientalist paintings—hence the magnificent cover of Said's *Orientalism*, exposing this particular penchant of the sexually arrested Orientalist. The cover of *Reading Lolita in Tehran* updates a long tradition in Orientalist painting and colonial postcards; Frederick Arthur Bridgman's "Algerian Girl" (1888) and his "Harem Girl" (date unknown) are its two most immediate ancestors, along with the whole genre of colonial picture postcards of young Algerian women—staged, produced and bought by French colonial officers. In his study of these colonially manufactured photographs, *The Colonial Harem* (1995), Malek Alloula has shown how the pathological colonial phantasm generated and sustained what Barthes called the "degree zero" of photographic evidence to represent and own the colonized body.[17] The Orientalists and the Oriental regiment of their native informers have every reason to hold the Orient at this infantile state. They rightly fear that when these boys reach adulthood they will grow beards or wear austere black cloaks. Likewise, when both the girls and boys fully mature they are quite likely to despise their imperial tormentors, expose their sexual perversion, and castrate their phallic claims to power.

This act of colonial provocation is not the end of what the cover of *Reading Lolita in Tehran* does. In fact, it provides an intriguing twist on Roland Barthes' binary opposition between the *denoted* and *connoted* messages of a photograph and its caption. The twist rests on the fact that the picture of these two teenagers is lifted from an entirely different context. It has absolutely nothing to do with teenagers reading a novel. It has been kidnapped from a news report filed during the parliamentary election of February 2000 and shows the young women reading the leading reformist newspaper, *Mosharekat*.

The cover of *Reading Lolita in Tehran* is thus an iconic burglary from the press, distorted and staged in a frame for an entirely different purpose than its original circumstance. The picture is cropped so that we no longer see the newspaper. Prior to the burglary, the two students were reading the results of a major parliamentary election, in which their national fate was being decided. Cropping out the newspaper to suggest that they were actually reading *Lolita* is, to say the very least, highly questionable.

FACT, FICTION AND FANTASY

To crop out a portion of reality in order to package a bigger lie is not just the story of the cover; it is the blueprint for the entire book. In the age of "the end of history", the function of the comprador intellectual is to oblige by wiping out all national histories and providing an entertaining story to fill the vacuum and so cover up the burglary. The content of *Reading Lolita in Tehran* thus matches its insidious cover; both serve its imperial context. History suspended, one searches the book in vain for even a single insight into the books and authors (*Lolita*, *The Great Gatsby*, Henry James, and Jane Austen) that hold the four chapters narratively together, or into the daily workings of the Islamic Republic.

Unbearable (at times rather embarrassing) details of Nafisi's personal daily chores punctuate interminable chitchat. *Reading Lolita in Tehran* is not literary criticism, political commentary, or personal memoir for anything more noble than an overfed and under-nourished mind. In the United States, suburban New Jersey is proverbial among Americans for the banality of a useless, wasteful, boring, and futile life. In chapter after chapter she weaves the vacuous ledger of her quotidian tasks, the real and perceived atrocities of the Islamic Republic, characters and plots from the "forbidden Western classics"—all in a self-congratulatory language that has nothing but contempt for her own culture and context and nothing but wide-eyed adulation for "Western classics".

The entirety of Iran as a nation, a culture, a society, a reality, fades out behind the tale of a self-indulgent diva very pleased with her heroic deeds and quixotic victories. The story of *Reading Lolita in Tehran* thus gradually mutates into a parable of a Snow White and her Seven Dwarves getting together to save a nation from its own evil—left to its own devices, it is understood, Iran cannot save itself.

Back in the real world, there is of course nothing either new or extraordinary about Iranians' reading world literature as an act of political defiance. This picture is cropped in a fashion similar to the visual burglary committed on the book's cover—stealing a part of the truth to tell a bigger lie. It is not only "the Western classics" that Iranians have read in political defiance of the tyrannies that over the centuries have ruled them—whether the Pahlavis (about whose atrocities Nafisi remains entirely silent) or the current clerics.

Great works of literature from around the world have long graced and enriched Iranian literary and political culture. The French Revolution of 1789 occasioned the exposure of Iranians to French and English literatures. The European revolutions of 1848 deeply appealed to expatriate Iranian intellectuals in Istanbul, a development that resulted in more translations from French and English. The Russian Revolution of 1917 did the same with Russian literature. The US occupation of Iran during World War II, the Vietnam War, and the Civil Rights movement brought exposure to American literature. The Latin American revolutions, the African anti-colonial movements, Indian anti-colonial nationalism, the Chinese Revolution, the Cuban Revolution, the student uprising in France—all are additional landmarks of Iranian exposures to world literature. There has also been plentiful exposure to modern Arabic literature in the aftermath of the European colonial occupation of Palestine and Nasserite nationalism.

There is rhyme and reason to Iranians' attraction to various world literatures. Nafisi is either ignorant of this historical fact or else she is hiding it; in either case she is cropping and framing this picture, shrinking it to a size that is useful for recycling English literature in sustaining a predatory empire built on the broken and bludgeoned back of peoples and their cultures. CliffsNotes on English-language literature at the service of Paul Wolfowitz—that is *Reading Lolita in Tehran* in a nutshell.

What is impossible to miss is the almost total absence of any sort of Iranian context, historical or otherwise. There is not a single word as to why millions of people poured into streets and risked (and often lost) their lives to topple one of the most savage military dictatorships in modern history. It is as if the sole purpose of the 1979 revolution had been to inconvenience Nafisi.

Millions of real Iranians grew up reading subversive works of literature from the four corners of the world, not just under the terror of Khomeini's reign, but also under the tyranny of the tyrant who came before him and about whose reign of terror she remains silent. What about generations of brutalized Iranians who were beaten and tortured because they were in possession of a text by Bertolt Brecht, Henrik Ibsen, Maxim Gorky, Arthur Miller, Jack London, or other names outside the provenance of Nafisi's intention to appease American neocons—Vladimir Mayakovsky, Nazım Hikmat, Pablo Neruda, Faiz Ahmad Faiz, Langston Hughes, Ahmad Shamlou, Mahmoud Darwish? Why distort the literary history of a people, deform their lived experiences, disfigure their emotive measures, twist the truth of who and where they are in their struggle for dignity, and thus project a warped and banal portrait of their moral universe?

ETHNIC CLEANSING WORLD LITERATURES

Criticizing the calamity of the Islamic Republic—and recognizing the heroism of a nation that first invested its hope in it and now is fighting it to the bitter end—is a legitimate and even urgent project. But shamelessly joining the neoconservative takeover of the democratic institutions of the United States by helping to build a literary canon for a predatory empire is an entirely different matter. The former restores dignity and hope to a nation and its national resistance to imperial domination; the latter seeks to steal such dignity and hope. Generations of Iranian women—political activists, avant-garde writers, pioneering poets, creative artists, and celebrated filmmakers—have put up a heroic resistance to the brutalities of their domestic patriarchy and the obscenities of the colonial gaze. Nafisi is not among them; she has betrayed them. From Tahereh Qorrat al-Ayn in the nineteenth century to Mehrangiz Kar in the twenty-first, Iranian woman have demanded and exacted their democratic rights and shown noble aspirations to freedom. The function of *Reading Lolita in Tehran* is to obliterate that empowering memory and make it subservient to American empire.

Was there nothing from Iranian culture itself that could save it: cinema, poetry, fiction? Did these Iranians—these damned, demented, dull, fanatical people for whom Nafisi has nothing but contempt and yet for whom she now speaks—did they not have an Austen, Fitzgerald, James, and Nabokov of their own? Forough Farrokhzad and Sohrab Sepehri were dead, but was their poetry buried with them? What about Ahmad Shamlou, Houshang Golshiri, Mahmoud Dolatabadi, Simin Daneshvar, Shahrnoush Parsipour, Simin Behbahani, Moniru Ravanipour, Mahshid Amirshahi—were they all dead, non-existent, expelled to obsolescence? Have the enthusiastic reviewers of *Reading Lolita in Tehran* ever wondered why this professor of literature not once—not once—refers to a work of literature in Persian in any shape or form (except in a nonsensical aside at the very end of the book to Iraj Pezeshkzad's *My Uncle Napoleon*), or why the only generic reference that she makes comes with the contemptuous sneer "the so-called realistic fiction coming out of Iran"? Did Iranians not have a literature of their own?

To Nafisi's upper-bourgeois, Swiss-boarding-school-sensitive nose, everything about Iran and Iranians is pungent and contemptible. Living comfortably in the midst of a misery for which her class was chiefly responsible, she roamed the streets of Tehran with a certain Jeff (an American journalist) at a time when thousands of poor Iranian students of a myriad of ideological persuasions were being slaughtered by one faction or another. The Islamic Revolution was and remains a poor people's revolution—with all the banalities, brutalities, stupidities, and yet unsurpassed hopes of a poor people's revolution. No human being ought to be forced to wear a garment she does not want to wear. But reading Nafisi it is impossible not to conclude that she and her class of whitewashed bourgeoisie hated the veil because it hid their class privileges from their poor compatriots.

It does not really matter how much of the story of the proverbial seven (neither six nor eight will do—either the cosmogonic seven or the apostolic twelve) students getting together with their wise and courageous teacher is true or fabricated. What matters is the cumulative effect of a consistently supercilious book and its success at mustering its author into the Oriental regiment of neocons in the post-9/11 nightmare we now inhabit. Nafisi may well have helped seven Iranian students survive the nightmare of Ayatollah Khomeini. But she and her book, along with people like Fouad Ajami, whom she thanks for having given her a job, and people like Bernard Lewis and Cynthia Ozick, who described the book as a "masterpiece" and indeed "glorious"—they are themselves the frightful creatures of a nightmare that the rest of us have to endure. Azar Nafisi may be able to think or sell herself in Washington DC as a heroic teacher who resisted a minor dinosaur, Ayatollah Khomeini, but she has placed herself and her book squarely in the service of a far more ferocious Tyrannosaurus Rex and thereby supported the terror that it is perpetrating around the globe.

ENGLISH IS THE ONLY LITERATURE

There is another, not so hidden agenda behind *Reading Lolita in Tehran*. Decades into a struggle against the domination of a Eurocentric curriculum in the American academy—what is, in effect, a fight to restore democratic dignity to the world literary scene— there appears an Iranian former professor of English literature singing the glories of "Western classics". Ignorant of, indifferent to, or opposed to projects for introducing progressive programs of comparative literature in the United States and Europe, or else dutifully performing a task for her neoconservative friends, Nafisi proclaims the "Western classics" the sole source of salvation for a Muslim nation. No one will ever know from *Reading Lolita in Tehran* that Iranians, like all other nations, have a literature of their own, that they are survivors in terms native to their own perils and promises, and that in the very same period that Nafisi was saving the souls of her seven students, Iranians were producing a glorious cinema that has captured the awe and admiration of the world, thus wresting the terms of their own dignity back from the tyrannical class that is now in charge of their destiny.

Never has the face of English literature been so repulsive. Emerging from *Reading Lolita in Tehran* you may find yourself detesting the authors Nafisi has dragged into the grime of this dirty service to empire. You will have to take a long shower—of a vastly different sort from the one she took when getting ready to receive her students—to wash from these works of art the scarring treacheries they have been subjected to in this horror of a book. Part of the repugnance of *Reading Lolita in Tehran* lies in Nafisi's utter ignorance of the massive debates in the academy over multi-culturalism, part in her having joined with the forces of resistance to curricular change.

Perhaps because Nafisi has never taught at any liberal-arts college or university in the United States, she appears entirely ignorant of the decades-long struggle that minorities (Native Americans, African-Americans, Latin Americans, Asian-Americans, gays and lesbians, and many more) have waged to make a dent in the vacuum-packed curriculum of the white establishment. She is, though brown, white-identified to the marrow of her bone. With utter disregard for the struggle of disenfranchised communities, Nafisi squarely places yet another non-European culture at the service not only of the empire's global insatiability but also of its domestic agenda.

THE ODDITY OF THE OTHER

Nafisi joined the chorus that demonizes resisting cultures and glorifies "the West" by writing about the oddity of reading *Lolita* in Tehran as if its reception in the United States and Europe had been smooth. The book and both its film adaptations were banned or boycotted after its original publication in France in 1955. Nabokov could not even find an American publisher willing to take a risk with *Lolita*; by 1954, at least four had turned him down. He finally took his book to Europe and consented to allow Maurice Girodias' Olympia Press—the publisher of such pornographic titles as *White Thighs*, *With Open Mouth*, and *The Sexual Life of Robinson Crusoe*—to publish only 5,000 copies. Until Graham Greene took *Lolita* seriously and published an interview with Nabokov, no one in Europe or the US was willing to review the book. Greene's endorsement outraged the British public. John Gordon, editor of *Sunday Express*, called *Lolita* "the filthiest book I have ever read" and "sheer unrestrained pornography".[18] The British Home Office ordered customs to confiscate all copies entering the United Kingdom and pressured the French minister of the interior to ban the book. In 1962, when Stanley Kubrick released his adaptation of *Lolita*, he faced the censorial policies of the Hollywood Production Code and the Roman Catholic Legion of Decency. Years later, in 1998, when Adrian Lyne's *Lolita* was released, it was skewered by the conservatives in both the United States and Europe. The 1994

Megan's Law in New Jersey, the Child Pornography Prevention Act of 1995, and the murder of JonBenet Ramsey in 1996 were all in hot public debate, casting the odds against Lyne. Even today, if conservatives were aware of the pedophiliac implications of *Reading Lolita in Tehran*, Nafisi's employment at the School of Advanced International Studies might be in jeopardy.

Ultimately, the catastrophe of this book hinges on the politics of its location—and the active uses to which its author's poverty of ideas has put it. Consequently, it has no real bearing on the horrors of the Islamic Republic and the atrocities it continues to perpetrate on the democratic aspirations of a nation. The very book you are now reading on the indecency of *Reading Lolita in Tehran*, if it were to be written in Persian and published in Tehran, would entice the Bernard Lewises and Cynthia Ozicks of the Islamic Republic (because these nightmares are not culture specific or exclusive to the United States) to praise it as a masterpiece, and national radio and TV shows would interview its author—inviting other lucrative offers his way. In the post-9/11 world, publishing conglomerates are eager to give you lucrative contracts to sit in Washington DC and write a book against an Islamic Republic. But the true test of our mettle is to live in Iran and speak the truth to those small dinosaurs who are running the country. Mirroring Nafisi in the United States, there are plenty of career opportunists in Iran who are defiling the United States on a daily basis for a high price. In Washington, DC, Azar Nafisi is the functional equivalent of the militant ideologues of the Islamic Republic, who side with power out of pure and simple careerism. Azar Nafisi did not choose her Muslim enemies carefully enough, for she has morphed into them.

THUS SPOKE THE ORIENTAL

Nafisi's most useful task has been as an Oriental voice accrediting the sole surviving Orientalist who has served both British colonialism and American imperialism in the span of a lifetime. (He is quite a museum piece.) Long before Bernard Lewis anointed *Reading Lolita in Tehran* a masterpiece, in what amounted to an infomercial on him published in *US News and World Report*, this is what Nafisi had to say about him:

"When I was studying in the States in the 1970s I was very much against people like Lewis. I had far more books by people like Said. When I went back and lived and taught in Tehran in 1979,

I began to discover how many of my assumptions were wrong."
Reading Lewis, she discovered, among other things, that Muslims
until the mid-nineteenth century had been far more critical of their
own culture than any Orientalist ever was—a self-critical spirit
that she had been ignorant of until Lewis and other "Orientalists"
led her to it.

It is of course difficult to guess exactly how many "people like
Said" Nafisi had in mind. But her crucial function as a comprador
intellectual is in accrediting the discredited Orientalist—and
"people like" him. After Edward Said dismantled the whole
edifice of Orientalism, Nafisi is recruited to reaccredit it. The
ridiculous disparity between these two citations—Edward Said and
Azar Nafisi—does not matter, because its absurdity has already
been facilitated by the banality of the parity proposed between
"people like Said" and "people like Lewis". For people like Lewis,
one Oriental is as good—or as disposable—as another. But in
anticipation of his endorsement, Nafisi makes sure that one of
the demonic characters she portrays in her book as an "Islamist
student" is an avid supporter of Said—thus identifying the most
celebrated public intellectual of his generation, the most eloquent
voice speaking against the terror of this empire, with the most
retrograde sentiments in a theocracy.

As for the substance of the endorsement of Lewis, Nafisi may
indeed be ignorant of any number of things—including Islamic
intellectual history. But to assume that, before Lewis and other
mercenary Orientalists told them so, Muslims were not aware of
their own self-critical spirit simply defies belief. How could Muslims
be self-critical of their own culture but not be aware that they have
been self-critical? The sheer inanity of the suggestion flies in the face
of reason and sanity. But the quotation from a self-loathing Oriental
confirming the structural hatred of a civilization across lands and
cultures pays back handsomely when Lewis returns the favor and
blurbs her book. Who is manipulating whom here? Who is Lolita
and who is Humbert Humbert?

Nafisi's activities continued after the publication of *Reading
Lolita in Tehran*. By the time Shirin Ebadi was awarded the Nobel
Peace Prize in 2003, the right-wing editorial pages of the *Wall Street
Journal* could rely on their Iranian native informer for a ghastly
piece turning the occasion into yet another spin in the war against
terrorism. Where else would the two leading native informers meet
but in the *Journal*'s illustrious pages—Ibn Warraq on Edward Said

and Nafisi on Shirin Ebadi? Nafisi abused Ebadi's reception of the Nobel Peace Prize in yet another cliché-ridden diatribe against the atrocities of the Islamic Republic, in a language that incites and invites her employers at the School of Advanced International Studies and the Pentagon to invade Iran and promote her ever higher. Perhaps she would ride into Tehran on a tank, in décolleté, holding Nabokov's *Lolita* and heralding freedom. Of one thing we can be sure: Shirin Ebadi did not earn the Nobel Prize she so richly deserved and joyously received by reading *Lolita* in Tehran.

4
The House Muslim

Here is our black man "who through his intelligence and hard work has hoisted himself to the level of European thought and culture," but is incapable of escaping his race ... Forgive us the expression, but Jean Veneuse [a self-loathing character in an African novel] is the man to be slaughtered. We shall do our best.

Frantz Fanon (1952)

The primacy of the knowing subject was paramount in both Fanon and Said's anti-colonial projects. Said predicated his own lifelong project on a recognition of Fanon's psychoanalytic of the entrapment in which colonial subjects find themselves, with their agential authorship in history nullified by the downcast European gaze; but he sought at the same time to reassert the human at the heart of literary humanism in a more global and democratic, consciously counter-colonial reading of world literatures. In order for us to do so, it is imperative to expand our understanding of world literature beyond such ecumenical German humanists as Goethe (who did in fact envision a universal Weltliteratur but from the vantage point of European humanism, not a democratic dialectic in which people and their literary masterpieces participated). What David Damrosch has also suggested, following Goethe—that world literature ought to be read as an "elliptical refraction"[1] of national literatures—still posits the idea of "world literature" as a reality sui generis and not as the democratically mobile constellation of the varied and thriving nuclei of polyvocal literatures in their original languages and cultures. It is only in the originary moment of literature, before it has been turned "elliptical" in world literature that the complication of the human can take place and enable a mode of agential autonomy beyond the power-basing assumption of "the West" and the rest.

If national and transnational literatures are thus to enter the global scene, then they ought to be first recognized in the cosmopolitan context of their originary production. One problem with existing notions of world literature is that they tend to pluck literary works out of this context and so disregard what Said called the specific worldliness of their hermeneutics, or what Gayatri Spivak calls their literary idiomaticity.[2] That context is a reality that cannot be reduced to any one of its constituent forces. When it comes to the literary works from Muslim lands of the past 1400 years, Islam is of course integral to their worldliness and idiomaticity but by no stretch of imagination definitive to them. The parochial triumphalism at the heart of American imperialism today, however, has advanced an imperial nativism that regards the cultures it faces (as friend or foe) as native, nativist, and—the instant it sees them at odds with its own universalizing nativism—peripheral.[3]

The principal achievement of the Orientalist project is the false binary opposition between Islam and the West which has made this particularly oppositional "Islam" definitive to the cultures in which it is embedded. Historically, however, Islam (itself a vastly cosmopolitan product of its many contexts) has of course always been integral to what is inevitably (but always with reservation) referred to as "Muslim societies" but never definitive to them. Over the past 200 years, the Orientalist project has reduced these multifaceted societies to Islam, and Islam to Islamic law (Shari'ah). In part because the Orientalists themselves were anything between pious and fanatical practitioners of their own religion (mostly Christianity), and in part because the capitalist modernity they were serving had posited itself as the Hegelian (rational) end of history in search of its pre-historical (irrational) moments, they went after the specifically doctrinal and juridical dimensions of the cultures they studied at the heavy cost of disregarding or dismissing their multicultural, polyvocal, artistic, literary, poetic, philosophical, and mystical dimensions—and to the degree that they did study these aspects they always reduced and gauged them in doctrinal and juridical terms entirely alien to their very raison d'être, foreign and in fact hostile to their innate hermeneutics of alterity.

True to the historic services they are now performing for their white masters, our native informers are particularly adamant in reducing both the historical and the contemporary polyvocality of Muslims to an essentialist conception of Islam, and then summarizing this Islam with a number of key iconic insignia (Prophet Muhammad and the Quran in particular); and then denouncing or ridiculing Muhammad and the Quran and seeking to embarrass Muslims at large by appealing to the superior authority of "the West" and Enlightenment modernity. The 10 million plus Muslims who live in the United States (about 3 percent of the total population) and the 20 million plus Muslims who live in Europe (about 5 percent of the total population) are the principal target, with the 1.5 billion

Muslims around the globe as a secondary target, mostly via the racist and imperial foreign policies of Europe and the United States. In any film, fiction, or "documentary" about Muhammad or the Quran one is almost certain to find these native informers—ex-Muslims, as they often proudly call themselves—ridiculing Muhammad and disparaging the Quran. What they are selling their white audiences has little to do with the realities of Muslim societies. They are creating a Muslim enemy (reduced to a few manufactured icons) they can dehumanize and subjugate by assuming a superior civilizing mission—before they begin dropping tons of bombs.

The best example of this particular brand of native informer is the very curious case of someone who calls himself "Ibn Warraq".

THE MAKING OF A SELF-LOATHING MUSLIM

A closer look at Ibn Warraq reveals a number of features coalescing to make this native informer particularly useful to his host country. Born into a Muslim society, but now bearing unsurpassed hatred for his own birth and breeding, Ibn Warraq is a highly representative case of self-loathing. He is reported to be a renegade Pakistani Muslim who found Western enlightenment and is now living in North America or Western Europe. Who can better lay out the maladies of a murderous religion than one who was once afflicted with it? Ibn Warraq is a curious case of a man who both personifies and persecutes the object of his loathing: he is the Muslim he abhors, the object of his own hatred. He takes particular pleasure in the admiration of racist Americans and Europeans, for within it dwells their hatred for Muslims and for Ibn Warraq himself, reflecting his own. It is exceedingly saddening to watch a person self-flagellate so pitilessly.

Autophobia—the affliction affecting the person who is both the subject and the object of his own hatred—assumes a more convoluted character when he offers himself as a person in absentia, a pseudonym. The ostensible reason for Ibn Warraq's anonymity is that were he to reveal his identity his life would be in danger—which is a joke, since the only people in danger in the West are those who openly criticize the criminal atrocities of American empire and European racism. Those who endorse them are, in contrast, rewarded, praised, and published.

Ibn Warraq's most important feature is his anonymity. He lives in hiding for fear of his life—so goes the fantasy—because the truths he reveals about Islam are so dangerous that Muslims would very much like to kill him; such, in any case, is the aura he has successfully manufactured around himself. Someone has actually recently come forward claiming to be Ibn Warraq. But there is no way of being sure that the claim is true. For all we know this person, too, might be a rogue, an opportunist trying to cash in on the notoriety Ibn Warraq has managed to create for himself. Herein, I will treat "Ibn Warraq" as the aggregate author of the books, articles, and interviews attributed to him, and for this purpose he remains the anonymity he has always been, an ignominy in hiding, a shame, a sham, an industry, a robot, a hologram, a native informer. That someone has now come forward to claim his identity does not resolve but, in fact, further complicates the labyrinthine anonymity of the character that calls itself "Ibn Warraq". For the sake of simplicity I will thus assume that (1) Ibn Warraq is just one person, not a pseudonymous designation for a cluster or an industry; and (2) that he is male—though we have no way of knowing, and I refer to him with masculine pronoun (and thus unwillingly humanize him) because I am forced by the rules of grammar to choose a gender, though he could also be a she or, more accurately, an it.

The corollaries of this manufactured anonymity are that (1) Ibn Warraq's ideas are revolutionary and dangerous, and (2) that Muslims are so far from ready to hear them they would murder him if they could. *The Wall Street Journal* concludes a major piece that it commissioned from Ibn Warraq (on the occasion of Edward Said's death in September 2003) by explaining that he uses a pseudonym "to protect himself and his family from Islamists"[4]—lending its own editorial voice to the conviction that something in Islam and Muslims is murderous (while if one is critical of US imperialism and Israeli colonialism one and one's family are perfectly safe and immune to any sort of harassments[5]).

Ibn Warraq's ruse conceals a long line of Muslims who have written courageously, imaginatively, and above all caringly against the atrocities in their own religion and culture, in Arabic, Persian, Urdu, or Turkish, and all under their own names. Throughout history, Muslim societies (like all other societies) have been afflicted with any number of pressing problems. Over a long and tumultuous history, Muslims have been divided into sects and factions by their convictions and proclivities. Like Jews, Christians, and Hindus, they have been at one another's throats since the time immemorial—jurists against theologians, theologians against philosophers, philosophers against mystics, revolutionaries against rulers, radicals against liberals against conservatives. All societies are organic entities, moved and divided by the animus of time and events. Singling Muslim societies out, with a renegade house Muslim going berserk over these problems in English for an audience foreign and at times even hostile, not only does nothing toward addressing and alleviating those problems but in fact puts expatriate Muslim communities in North America and Western Europe, Ibn Warraq's primary targets, on the defensive while aiding and abetting racist Europeans and Americans in their contempt for the newest phase of immigration that brings yet another colored wave from their former colonies to their shores.

Alongside the mixture of autophobia and anonymity that gives Ibn Warraq an air of abstract authority—the voice of an omniscient narrator—is a case of self-delusional megalomania. Ibn Warraq has successfully marketed himself as the very first secular Muslim intellectual to dare question the tenets of the faith. The following exchange took place in a 2001 interview on an Australian radio station:

> Stephen Crittenden: What's implied behind all that is that Islam is potentially going to be required, maybe by the West, to go through something a bit like the Reformation that the Christian church went through.
>
> Ibn Warraq: Exactly, and that's why, as I've said over and over again, it is illogical, totally illogical, for the Western media, there's an editorial practically every month now in *The Times*, which laments the lack of a Reformation within Islam, and then to ignore books like mine. How do they think [the]Reformation's going to come about?
>
> Stephen Crittenden: Of course if that's so, we're talking about one of the biggest stories in the history of religion!
>
> Ibn Warraq: Right. I mean this might seem a bit megalomaniac. But it's got to start somewhere.[6]

What we have here is a native informer claiming extraordinary powers of representation as an exceptional case that proves the rule, a self-delusional ego that is in fact quite conscious of being megalomaniac. Ibn Warraq now produces one hefty book after another on whatever he wishes: the history of the writing of the Quran, the character of Muhammad, the history of early Islam, the Salman Rushdie scandal, the status of women in Islam, the archaic nature of Islamic law, the absence of human rights in Islamic societies.[7]

Reviewers even more colorful than Ibn Warraq praise him as the first Muslim ever to criticize the faith and defend the West.[8] Taking advantage of a widespread public ignorance about anything Islamic on the one hand, and a publicly irrelevant academic discourse that knows more and more about less and less on the other, Ibn Warraq has flooded the market with books selling himself as the "secular reformer" who will take the first step toward reforming Islam from within, although no one knows whether he resides within or outside Islam. The truth, of course, is that from the time of Muhammad to the present every single aspect of the faith (beginning with the divine origin of the Quran and the sanctity of Muhammad's message) has been challenged, questioned, overridden, reinterpreted, counter-interpreted, discarded, and reasserted by Muslims themselves; absolutely nothing in the cliché-ridden utterances of Ibn Warraq is new to a Muslim ear, except, perhaps, for the self-loathing that makes one a bit uneasy to be in the presence of a writer so disgusted with himself. But the self-loathing and the megalomania further complicate the abstracted knot that sustains the anonymity of this native informer.

All of which ultimately transmutes into an unabashed racism that defies even Malcolm X's characterization of "the house negro". Ibn Warraq's hatred of what he calls "the Arabs" comes out especially when he faces a Christian interlocutor, as in the following exchange:

Stephen Crittenden: Is one of the key problems that Islam faces, its Arabic tribal origins? Christianity was a cosmopolitan religion from the word go, Judaism was forced to become one. Is Islam a kind of attempt though at one level, to sort of transform the whole world into an Arabic tribe?

Ibn Warraq: Oh yes, that is the agenda of political Islam, if you like, if you can call it that. But within Islam generally, there has been this current that says that Islam is the perfect religion, the prophet was the last of the prophets, and it is the duty of every Muslim to bring this religion to the whole of humanity. There is a certain logic in that, it's not my logic because I don't accept their premise.[9]

... Anyway, coming back to multiculturalism, we cannot hope to have a civic society if we do not value the same things, if we do not pursue the same goals, and we cannot do this if we keep emphasizing the differences. We must have a shared core of values, and it seems essential that we get beyond this divisive multiculturalism, which essentially means Western bashing, bashing the West, we will not get anywhere until we emphasize the things that we value, like separation of church and state, liberalism, democracy, the value of rationality, discussing our problems and so on. And yet our leaders have been incredibly remiss. They pour even more money into keeping people apart. It seems insane to me. Instead of teaching the new arrivals and new immigrants the language of the host community, mostly English in Britain of course, and in America and Australia, they're spending thousands of dollars and pounds on encouraging language teaching in Punjabi, in Urdu, in Hindi, it seems completely daft; how on earth can these people integrate and become a part of the community if they do not speak the language of that community?[10]

The only way such a person can be so unbridled and open in his racism toward his own people is by having metaphorically replaced his collective identity with his individual persona. The man detests himself; he projects that loathing toward a generalized 'other', of which he is a member, so that he can express his hatred toward himself with impunity.

As an act of masochistic pleasure, this self-directed racism seeks the widest possible publicity to expose and stage itself. To attain that publicity, Ibn Warraq (like many other comprador intellectuals) has found it expedient to focus his rage on Edward Said, whose position as a prominent intellectual offers prominence to his antagonists. Days after the death of Said, on September 25, 2003, *The Wall Street Journal* published Ibn Warraq's opinion piece on him. (It is quite strange how easy editors find it to contact this man who is in hiding for his life.) Under a catchy subtitle—"The man who gave us the intellectual argument of Muslim rage dies"—Ibn Warraq proceeded to suggest that Said:

> will go down in history for having practically invented the intellectual argument for Muslim rage. "Orientalism", his bestselling manifesto, introduced the Arab world to victimology. The most influential book of recent times for Arabs and Muslims, "Orientalism" blamed Western history and scholarship for the ills of the Muslim world: Were it not for imperialists, racists and Zionists, the Arab world would be great once more. Islamic fundamentalism, too, calls the West a Satan that oppresses Islam by its very existence. "Orientalism" lifted that concept, and made it

over into Western radical chic, giving vicious anti-Americanism a high literary gloss.[11]

Ibn Warraq accused Said of being "the most influential exponent of ... a powerful philosophical predicate for Islamist terrorism" and called Orientalism "a polemic that masqueraded as scholarship. Its historical analysis was gradually debunked by scholars". Moreover, he has said: "Mr Said routinely twisted facts to make them fit his politics. For example, to him, the most important thing about Jane Austen's *Mansfield Park* was that its heroine, Fanny Price, lived on earnings from Jamaican sugar—imperialist blood money". Ibn Warraq's judgment was thus foregone:

> In his writings, verbal allusion and analogy stood in for fact, a device to reassure the ignorant of the correctness of his conclusions. Of these he found many over the years in American universities. His works had an aesthetic appeal to a leftist bent of mind, but even this now can be seen as a fad of the late twentieth century. The irony, of course, is that he was ultimately grandstanding for the West—for Western eyes, Western salons, and Western applause.[12]

This astoundingly illiterate reading of Said, this deliberate distortion of his thought, requires closer examination, for it cannot be explained entirely by the native informers' proclivity to endear themselves to the Zionist contingency, although that factor does seem to figure as a crucial incentive for Ibn Warraq, Nafisi, and Fouad Ajami, among many others. But something more serious in the case of Ibn Warraq requires patient unpacking.

For an answer we need to look at the politics of the spectacle. The most vital and spectacular events of the last part of the twentieth century and the first decade of the twenty-first have involved Islam and Muslims. With the continuing saga of the Palestinian dispossession from the middle of the century, the simultaneous partition of India along a Muslim-Hindu divide, and the anti-colonial movements waged against European powers throughout the world, Muslim societies have all but defined global geopolitics. The Islamic Revolution in Iran (1977–79) and the eight bloody years of the Iran-Iraq War (1980–88) commenced the most recent phase of global geopolitics, in which oil has been the defining economic factor in the significance of the region ranging from the Indian Ocean to the Arabian Sea, the Persian Gulf, the Levant, and all the way to North Africa. The Soviet invasion and occupation of Afghanistan (1978–88), the American hostage crisis (1979–80), the Salman Rushdie affair (1989), the first Gulf War (1990–91), the carnage of two successive Intifadas (1987–93 and 2000–03), and the repeated invasions and occupations of Lebanon (1982–2006) culminated in the spectacular events of 9/11/01 and the subsequent US-led invasions of Afghanistan (October 2001) and Iraq (March 2003). The insatiable thirst of the native informers for publicity is the product of these environments.

These developments have coincided with the phenomenon Guy Debord diagnosed in 1967 as *The Society of the Spectacle* (*La Société du spectacle*), in which a widespread commodity fetishism has moved into the age of globalized mass media and endemic alienation has metastasized into the absolute visuality of everyday life. The native informers demonstrate the factual dementia of reality, the overcoming of facts by visual fantasy upon a spectacular stage where the self-loathing Muslim partakes in and mutates into the image of Islam that has taken root in the globally alienated mind. The more outrageously the native informers can posit this dangerous Islam as the enemy of the humanity at large, the better they will have inhabited the collective psyche of the global hatred they at once invite and welcome. Through this mental metempsychosis, the native informers become the collective consciousness of the race and the faith they at once personify and loath.[13]

As particularly acute cases of Islamophobia, Ibn Warraq and Hirsi Ali represent native informers who at once inhabit and target, personify and alienate, the hated abstraction they wish to exorcise from the moral psychosis that has posited them as aliens. The native informers thus identify with white hatred, but in order to be able to go on living they project this hatred onto their collective identity and away from their hidden and anonymous I—thus the evident paradox of both self-loathing and megalomania. The difference between Ibn Warraq and Hirsi Ali is that while her hatred for her own collective identity remains abstract and hidden within the stories that she keeps weaving about her life, his coagulates around the public figure of Edward Said, and by performing a character assassination—he perpetrates what he says he is afraid of; he assassinates the character that he says he hates but in fact envies and emulates.

He does to Said's character what he says he is afraid will be done to his own body. This ultimately is a death-wish on the part of the native informer, for by negatively identifying with Said and yet assassinating his character (when he is already dead) he seeks to become equally famous and prominent in the moment of his own self-abrogation—a pathology that is perhaps best captured in cinema in the psychotic figure of Travis Bickle (Robert DeNiro) in Martin Scorsese's *Taxi Driver* (1976), who thinks that by assassinating the widely popular Senator Palantine he can finally find a public persona. In his psychotic oscillations between autophobia and anonymity, self-loathing and megalomania, Travis Bickle anticipates Ibn Warraq.

WHY IS HE NOT A MUSLIM?

Who is a native informer and what does he do—and how does he cover his brown skin with a white mask? My preliminary sketch of Ibn Warraq as a self-loathing Muslim must be augmented by a closer look at his manner of professing that he thinks he is no longer a Muslim—a gambit that makes him particularly useful to his supporters and endorsers in North America and Western Europe. Why is he not a Muslim, he wants you to wonder—and why, one may add, should anyone care? The peculiar combination of self-loathing and megalomania that results in targeting Edward Said for character assassination seems to seek an almost identical notoriety in the realm of political violence—an astounding audacity that makes him the functional equivalent of Muhammad Atta, the alleged mastermind behind the 9/11 attacks, in their common proclivity to ram violently into towering edifices.

In his first book, *Why I Am Not a Muslim* (1995), Ibn Warraq writes of having been born in a non-Arabic-speaking Muslim country: "Even before I could read or write the national language I learned to read the Koran in Arabic without understanding a word of it."[14] He still does not know a word of Arabic, he confesses, which did not prevent him from editing *The Origins of the Koran* (1998), *The Quest for the Historical Muhammad* (2000), and *What the Koran Really Says* (2002). What would we think of a scholar who understood no Hebrew yet wrote voluminously on the historical character of Moses and the Hebrew Bible; or who knew no Aramaic yet wrote a biography of Jesus; or who knew no Sanskrit yet issued two volumes on the Bhagavad-Gita?

The vulgarity, the chutzpah! In *Why I Am Not a Muslim* Ibn Warraq confesses that until the fatwa against Salman Rushdie in 1989 he had not been much of an author. (He is reported to have run an Indian restaurant in France before becoming an Islamic scholar in the United States.) It was the Rushdie affair that propelled him to expose the atrocities of Muslims, the criminal foundations of Islam, and the constitutional inability of Muslims to catch up with modernity.

Mixed with this vulgar audacity is a brazen exhibitionism, an obvious pleasure in flaunting his outrages. It is as though he had conducted a study of the most obnoxious things European and American Orientalists have said about Islam, then looked into the most racist recent Islamophobic utterances, and then either quoted them or reprocessed them in his own prose. "I am not a scholar or a specialist," he explains, before going on to declare Bernard Lewis "one of the great prose writers of English of the last fifty years—elegant, urbane, and subtle" and to thank Daniel Pipes for his scholarship; and then to resurrect the decayed corpses of the most outlandish Orientalists of the past two hundred years for a danse macabre.[15] Ibn Warraq resuscitates the darkest moments of Orientalist racism, taking particular pleasure in denying his own ancestral faith and culture, his people and parentage—in other words, himself. We are in the presence of a Muslim masochist.

But what, exactly, is Ibn Warraq teaching his readers? He divides Islam into no less than three Islams:

Islam 1 is what the Prophet taught, that is, his teachings as contained in the Koran. Islam 2 is the religion as expounded, interpreted, and developed by the theologians through the traditions (Hadiths); it includes the Sharia and Islamic law. Islam 3 is what Muslims actually did do and achieved, that is to say, Islamic civilization.[16]

From this earth-shattering taxonomy Ibn Warraq unleashes the most vicious screeds ever uttered about Islam and the Arabs, concluding that the best that Islam 3 has produced actually came from non-Arabs and non-Muslims.[17] Having thoroughly internalized Orientalist delusions and European racism, he becomes a willing and able parrot repeating them for his own masochist pleasure.

There is a point where audacity plunges into stupidity.[18] Ibn Warraq spends the entirety of his first chapter, "The Rushdie Affair", going through a catalogue of Muslim thinkers, from Ibn Kammunah in the thirteenth century to Ali Dashti in the twentieth—courageous intellectuals who challenged, ridiculed, mocked, and denigrated aspects of their own religion—only to conclude that while Christians have succeeded in challenging the doctrinal foundations of their faith, "Muslims have yet to take even this first step". Here we need to set aside the question whether it is out of ignorance or malice that Ibn Warraq forgets centuries of European wars and massacres that forced millions to flee to another continent and millions more to steal another people's land so that they could be safe from these civilized Christians' pogroms and gas chambers. The more pressing question is, what malady could cause a writer to introduce a group of Muslim intellectuals who have done exactly what he claims no one before him ever did?

In his tenth chapter, Ibn Warraq delivers another catalogue of Muslims—mystics, philosophers, and scientists—who have categorically denied the Quranic revelation. Then what is he doing in English that Muslim intellectuals have not done for centuries and continue to do today in Arabic, Persian, Turkish, or Urdu, with their own names proudly adorning their writing—and above all with an unfailing love for the people who share their destiny? Ibn Warraq is nothing more than a court jester, flailing his motley and bells to amuse his fantasies of the White House and the Pentagon.

Ibn Warraq spends a good chunk of his first chapter discussing *Twenty-Three Years (Bist-o-Seh Sal)*, a famous book by the prominent Iranian public intellectual Ali Dashti, on the life of Muhammad, noting its radical critique of Islamic doctrine. Yet the basis of his information about Dashti is a secondary source, a book by Daniel Pipes, who himself cannot read the language in which Dashti's book was written, Persian (or, for that matter, Arabic), on the occasion of the Rushdie affair. Why rely on Pipes's book instead of the original? Because Ibn Warraq, like Pipes, cannot read Persian. Ali Dashti wrote it in the language of his fellow Iranians and published it in Iran long before these two monolinguals could pick up an English translation of it and weave it into a treacherous narrative to service the moral bankruptcy of an impotent empire.

In chapter after chapter, Ibn Warraq takes a perverse pleasure in recounting the ugliest European assertions about Islam. Dante, Hobbes, Voltaire, Hume, Gibbon, and Carlyle are paraded one after the other. *Why I Am Not a Muslim* is not, however, a merely malicious resuscitation of old-fashioned Orientalist knowledge production; the discipline had already succumbed under the weight of its racist and positivist incoherence and from the concurrent rise of the epistemic and hermeneutic revolutions, long before Said delivered his magnificent coup de grace. The colonial project is no longer operative; the political economy of the capital that once necessitated Orientalism as a system of colonial knowledge has long since shifted gear to a new propaganda machinery.

Ibn Warraq's demonization of his ancestral faith has, of course, nothing to do with an intellectual history wrought by schisms and sectarian divisions, moral defiance and political contestation—cutting deeply into the very core of Quranic revelation and Muhammadan charismatic mission. Muslims, like the adherents of any other world religion, have agreed and disagreed, celebrated their faith and contested its doctrines, challenged the metaphysical veracity of their culture and enriched its ethical dexterity; they have narrated their faith in juridical terms, then turned around and speculated about their religion theologically, before opposing both proclivities mystically, thus exploring the boundaries of reason and revelation. Muslims have produced a record of literary humanism in Arabic, Persian, Urdu, and Turkish unparalleled in medieval history. In art and architecture, science and technology, literature and poetry, Muslims have generated and sustained a world civilization. They have also systematically dismantled their own intellectual history to transform their faith into the site of ideological resistance to colonialism. Ibn Warraq is ignorant of the very texture and disposition of Islamic intellectual and doctrinal history.

His books summon an outlandish combination of challenges that Muslims themselves have posited within their own faith, misrepresenting their epistemic and historic disposition, adding some of the most hateful assertions about Arabs and Muslims (recycling European racist and anti-Semitic clichés about Africans and Jews), appending a mixed bag of Orientalist scholarship, and mixing it all to concoct a potion of self-loathing Orientalism that he places squarely at the service of a servile conception of "the West". As I have already said, the native informer does not tell the white master what he needs to know but what he wants to hear. In the case of Ibn Warraq (followed closely by that of Ayaan Hirsi Ali), the native informer personifies what the white master wants to loath.

Ibn Warraq thinks he is being blasphemous, but he is too meager a figure to be blasphemous. Blasphemy (kofr) is definitive to what Muslims over the centuries have considered faith (Iman)—but who is to explain this truth to Ibn Warraq's audience? You want blasphemy? Read Omar Khayyam—and you will learn the meaning of a noble faith.

ORIENTALISM OF THE ORIENTAL

Soon after he told us why he is not a Muslim, Ibn Warraq turned to the Quran. In *The Origin of the Koran* (1998), a collection of Orientalist treatises on the Muslim holy text, he indulges once again in passing along the worst Orientalist idiocies he can lay his hands on: Carlyle dismissing the Quran as "insupportable stupidity", Salomon Reinach opining that "It is humiliating to the human intellect to think that this mediocre literature has been the subject of innumerable commentaries, and that millions of men are still wasting time absorbing it".[19] Among the myriad scholarly works by Muslims and non-Muslims that have focused on the main contours of early Islamic history, Ibn Warraq singles out the outlandish Hagarism: *The Making of the Islamic World* (1977) by two born-again British Orientalists, Michael Cook and Patricia Crone, a book almost unanimously dismissed by serious historians of early Islam, to add yet another pinch of salt to the wound he has already inflicted.

It pleases Ibn Warraq tremendously that Cook and Crone argue that Islam is really an offshoot of a Jewish messianic movement. Their theory was almost immediately dismissed by other historians, partly because it is predicated on the mad notion that Muslims have spent centuries misrepresenting their own history, partly because in its essence it is both racist and anti-Semitic in its fantasy of an early Jewish conspiracy against Christianity. Both in its original formulation and in Ibn Warraq's malign reiteration, the bizarre argument is that later Islamic sources have fabricated an early history for Islam and hidden the fact that their faith is really nothing but a Judaic messianic cult invented to dislodge Christianity. In reality, of course, both Islam and Christianity are, in their very essence, rooted in Judaic prophetic tradition, but not as a result of delusional conspiracies of the sort that Cook and Crone dreamed up and Ibn Warraq passes along with evident glee.

Neither discussion of the Judaic roots of Islam nor the association of both these world religions with various messianic movements in the region is new or revolutionary. The figure of Abdullah ibn Saba, a Jewish convert to Islam, for example, has always been affiliated with the rise of the Shi'i branch of Islam, by far the most messianic tendency evident in the faith. There is no blasphemy Ibn Warraq can produce that does not already have a long and rather varied Islamic social and intellectual history. The problem with the Orientalist mummies he brings back to life is their ignorance of their own obsolescence—except to the bewildered American generals who keep inviting Bernard Lewis to advise them on empire building. Here, too, Ibn Warraq's hatred for Said echoes in the pleasure he takes in parading one Orientalist antiquity after another.

I have long maintained that Said's apt and overdue critique of Orientalism has been wrongly fetishized in his person and politics; what is important is his criticism of a particularly nasty mode of knowledge production. Long before he wrote his groundbreaking *Orientalism*, before Michel Foucault unearthed the relationship between knowledge and power, a sustained tradition in the sociology of knowledge had already shown that the creative consciousness of the individual is socially formed and collectively cadenced—and thus without a socially predicated prejudice and power no mode of knowledge is possible.[20] Said and his *Orientalism* have now become such iconic references that neo-Orientalists and their native informers think they need only knock him down a few pegs in order to be free to resume their inanities—because they have no clue as to where the power of the case against the Orientalists originates.

It is unfortunate that all the theoretical reflections predating the publication of *Orientalism* in 1978 have been subsumed under its peak; except for very limited academic circles, the public at large knows little of their contour and character. As early as the 1920s, Max Scheler and Karl Mannheim had commenced a major theoretical movement in the sociology of knowledge that radically revised our conception of the modes and modalities of knowledge production.[21] Before them, Wilhelm Jerusalem, who first coined the expression Soziologie des Erkenntniss in a 1909 essay, began a serious examination of the way the epistemic assumption of knowledge production is socially predicated and economically grounded. Both Scheler and Mannheim traced the origin of their sociology of knowledge to Karl Marx's *German Ideology* (1845), particularly to the way he had located the ideological presumptions of consciousness. Sociologists have detected similar bents in Max Weber's *The Protestant Ethic and the Spirit of Capitalism* (1904), Wilhelm Dilthey's *Essence of Philosophy* (1907), Emile Durkheim's *Sociology and Philosophy* (1924), and the papers of Charles Sanders Peirce (1839–1914), especially the collection in his *Pragmatism and Pragmaticism*.[22] There is also a tradition in the sociology of knowledge that links the European trait of the discipline to that of the pre-eminent American sociologist George Herbert Mead (1863–1931).[23] At the root of this theoretical investigation into the social and economic basis of knowledge production was what Max Weber identified as Verstehendesoziologie ("interpretative sociology"), by means of which he radically discredited the positivist tradition in the understanding of any social action and sought to prepare the groundwork for a hermeneutic sociology that explained the social behavior of individuals in terms domestic to their manner of understanding their own social behavior.[24]

The publication of Hans George Gadamer's *Truth and Method* (1960) expanded the field into an even more exciting and fruitful domain of hermeneutics and, through a detailed philosophical discussion, posited the historicity of consciousness and the contingency of the human subject—and thus dealt a mortal blow to any remnant notion of positivist knowledge.[25] Predicated on this long and sustained premise, Michel Foucault's articulation of the relationship between modes of power and manners and discourses of knowledge production was articulated and handed over to Edward Said.

Whereas Foucault traced the insidious modes of power basing at the roots of a variety of social practices and discourse formations, Said imploded these theoretical insights into a single sustained reflection on the nature of colonial power and the necessary mode of knowledge that corresponds to its political predicates. In *Discipline and Punish* (1975), Foucault detected the insidious panoptic mechanism of power whereby the human subject is "automatized" and "disindividualized" and thus "becomes the principle of his own subjection".[26] Whereas Foucault navigated the social formations of power in institutions and discourses domestic to a society, Said extended its discursive mechanism to a colonial relation of power between two polar ends of domination. The significance of *Orientalism* lies in its lifting a brilliant history of theoretical reflection on the correspondence between social institutions, economic forces, cultural practices, and modes of knowledge production to the pronounced political project of colonialism. The power of his formulation among his own contemporaries was so overwhelming that it overshadowed all these preceding reflections on the nature of knowledge and power—a collective amnesia that can be traced to the depoliticized practice of sociological theory, especially in the American academy.

Hence this entire iceberg of sustained theoretical reflection is hidden under the tip of Said's *Orientalism*, and not even its devoted admirers go beyond Foucault in their archeology of its insights—let alone its superficial detractors.[27] Cook and Crone are the belated leftovers of a manner of knowledge production that was deliberately designed to deny and denigrate a people and their literary and scholastic culture. Systematically denigrating Arabic sources in their Hagarism nonsense, they effectively inform an entire civilization that it is predicated on a false religion and a historical lie. And if few in the academy took that idea seriously, their reception was different in a world under siege, desperate for a mode of knowledge that heals wounds rather than adds insult to injury—and if the space for doing so is left open to charlatans like Ibn Warraq, then we are headed for catastrophes much worse than what George W. Bush inflicted on Afghanistan and Iraq and his Israeli counterparts on Palestine and Lebanon.

WHAT IS MUHAMMAD TO HIM OR HE TO MUHAMMAD?

Why bother with this self-loathing "Oriental"? Because what is at stake is the categorical dehumanization of a people marked as the enemy, a designation that native informers like Ibn Warraq are actively encouraged to personify, becoming both the accented voice of a subhuman enemy and the voice loathing it. If the matter were limited to a single person doing and receiving the loathing it would of course merit no serious attention. But that is not the case.

At this point, it is worth considering the Israeli army's massive military operation against Palestinians in Gaza that ran from Christmas 2008 to the New Year of 2009. Israeli F-16 bombers pounded the Gaza Strip, killing hundreds of Palestinians, mostly civilians, many of them women and children; hundreds more Palestinians, BBC News reported, were wounded. The medical staff at the main hospital in Gaza reported that their operating rooms were overflowing, that the hospital was running out of medicine, and that there were simply not enough physicians to cope with the crisis. According to BBC News, "Israel hit targets across Gaza, striking the territory's main population centres, including Gaza City in the north and the southern towns of Khan Younis and Rafah."

Meanwhile, BBC News continued, "US Secretary of State Condoleezza Rice accused Hamas of having triggered the new bout of violence … The United States is deeply concerned about the escalating violence in Gaza … We strongly condemn the repeated rocket and mortar attacks against Israel and hold Hamas responsible for breaking the ceasefire and for the renewal of violence there." Such was the official US reaction to what BBC News reports said was "the worst attack in Gaza since 1967 in terms of the number of Palestinian casualties".[28] But Israel refused a ceasefire and, according to its officials, intended to "change the facts on the ground".

Look at the following headline, which the *New York Times* ran hours after the Israeli strike against Palestinians commenced: "Israeli Gaza Strike Kills More Than 200." You might well ask "200 what?"

Could it be 200 Martians, Swedes, cats, dogs, mules, or ants? Where is the word "Palestinians"? Some 200 Palestinians—men, women, and children, young and old—had just been slaughtered. Did the dead not at least deserve to be identified as Palestinians? Instead, the *New York Times* immediately added, "Airstrikes on Hamas Sites Are a Response to Rocket Fire."[29] The same with CNN: "Israeli air attacks on Gaza kill 155." Nothing qualified that "155"; it could have been 155 geese, monkeys or ducks that the Israelis had killed. It was the same with the *Washington Post*: "Israeli War Planes Target Hamas Compounds; Attacks destroy dozens of security compounds, in unprecedented waves of air strikes; reports of at least 145 dead and hundreds wounded in Gaza." Again, no "Palestinians", just numbers. Why? Whence this omission or erasure of the word "Palestinian"—these people's humanity, their personhood, the blood and bone of the human beings that US-provided Israeli F-16 jets and Apache helicopters had wiped off the face of Palestine?

Why is it that the nouns Palestine and Palestinians are so consistently excised from the sites of their systematic destruction, dispossession, and massacre? Who and what are responsible for this elimination of the very name of a people? Why did the *New York Times* not say that 200 Palestinians had just been murdered by the Israeli army? Can you imagine what the *New York Times'* headline would have been if 200 Jews had been killed, and 300 Jews wounded—by Palestinians, or by Muslims? What animates this monstrosity? How can anyone live here without succumbing to anger, as Americans, as immigrants, as human beings, as citizens of a country whose Secretary of State had just blamed the victims of a brutal rape for causing it? It is reported that Palestinians have launched rockets at Israel that have caused a handful of deaths and injuries—a handful too many. Meanwhile, 1.5 million Palestinians in Gaza are being choked to death on a daily basis by an Israeli blockade that the United Nations calls a crime against humanity.[30] When a rapist is choking a woman and she screams and kicks and strikes out, can you say to the world, "Look! She is kicking me?" The Israeli defense minister, Ehud Barack, has quoted President Barack Obama, referring to the homemade rockets that Palestinians hurl at southern Israel, to the effect that "if rockets were being fired at his home while his two daughters were sleeping, he would do everything he could to prevent it".[31] Really? And what would Obama do if he had to bury his two daughters with his own hands, as Palestinian parents have done for more than 60 years? What would he do if he were a Palestinian father in Gaza and he had just come home from burying them after the Israeli bombing of their home? Why are such obvious points lost on these fine and civilized people—and what is the role of Ibn Warraq and his cohorts in this systematic, consistent, enduring, and endemic dehumanization of Arabs and Muslims?

It is only the American and Israeli mass media that systematically excise the name "Palestinians" from the massacres perpetrated on them. Even the supposedly liberal *Ha'aretz* was entirely fixated on "the operation": "IDF to mobilize 6,500 reservists for Gaza op: IDF deploys tanks and ground troops along Gaza border"—such was its lead headline two days into the Palestinian massacre, followed by "Two Katyusha rockets hit Ashdod area, Gaza militants' furthest target yet: Woman wounded in rocket strike on Ashkelon, four more rockets strike Eshkol region in west Negev".[32] As Palestinians are being massacred by the hundreds, the wounding of one Israeli woman (one too many) is more important to *Ha'aretz* than the murders of hundreds of Palestinians by the Israeli army. "The only blood that matters to me is Jewish blood!"—so says Steve (Daniel Craig) in Steven Spielberg's *Munich* (2005), as he and his Israeli comrades go around assassinating Palestinians. What is the difference between Jewish blood and Muslim blood? They are the same: human blood is human blood. Shedding it is an abomination, a crime, a sin, an insanity. Why is this not recognized and what is the role of Ibn Warraq and his cohorts in facilitating the assumption that Muslim blood is worthless?

At least two major European news outlets did repeatedly use the word "Palestinians" when reporting the massacre. BBC News reported on the front page of its website: "Massive Israeli air raids on Gaza; Air strikes kill more than 200 Palestinians in the Gaza Strip, medics say, as Israel targets Hamas militants with the heaviest raids on Gaza for decades."[33] Likewise, the *Financial Times* reported: "Israel launches fierce air strikes on Gaza: Israel attacks 30 sites across the Hamas-controlled Gaza Strip, killing at least 225 Palestinians, injuring hundreds more and raising the prospect of massive retaliation."[34] I will not even raise objections to the BBC's use of the wording "Hamas militants", its granting the Israeli colonial settlement the status of a democratic state but describing Palestinians who have gone to voting booths and elected Hamas as their representatives as "militants". The most one can hope for at this point is not balance but simply the acknowledgement of the humanity of the Palestinians, that they are not "200" but "200 Palestinians"—bleeding, bones broken, injured, murdered, buried, mourned, and soon to be revenged: Palestinians. And who is to tell them not to avenge themselves? If you prick them do they not bleed? And if you wrong them, shall they not seek revenge?

In reviewing such events, one must suppress one's feelings about Ibn Warraq's writings, and about all the other native informers in part responsible for having dehumanized Arabs and Muslims so successfully that Americans do not think twice before deleting the word "Palestinians" from the number of their dead. I must now patiently dissect Ibn Warraq's words in order to see through the mechanism that links them to the carnage. Back to Ibn Warraq: that is my intifada.[35]

The *Quest for the Historical Muhammad* (2000) is yet another collection of essays and chapters by old and new Orientalists, including the perennial French favorite Ernest Renan. None of these collected writings is unknown or even controversial. By and large, they represent the gamut of Orientalist scholarship on the life of the Prophet of Islam—some laudatory, others defamatory of his character and culture, others serious attempts at historical insight. The problem with this book is the material Ibn Warraq cherry-picks for citation, with a commitment to what he calls "Western scientific scholarship"—thereby implying that Muslims have no such capabilities. Ibn Warraq insists that while Muslims have failed to produce any objective account of their prophet's life (just a few pages after he has referred to Ali Dashti), the Orientalists have succeeded in doing so. He is dismissive of scholars he considers to have been coy in their critical apparatus for fear of offending Muslims; he insists that "Western scholars need to unflinchingly, unapologetically defend their right to examine Islam, to explain the rise and fall of Islam by normal mechanisms of human history, according to objective standards of historical methodology".[36] In other words only Western scholars can rescue Muslims from their historical ineptitude, hagiographical fantasies, and superstitious delusions.

Lost on both Ibn Warraq and his sponsors is the fact that writers produce biographies and hagiographies of their saints, prophets, and heroes in accordance with the specificities of their social circumstances—and that this is not a peculiarity exclusive to Muslims. In his extraordinary study of the figure of Jesus, Jaroslav Pelikan, the distinguished historian of Christian dogma, has demonstrated the variety of ways in which Christ has been historically reconfigured, from a Jewish rabbi to a Latin American revolutionary.[37] Muslims, too, have imagined a life of their prophet and other saintly figures compatible with their changing historical circumstances.[38] No biography is objective in any perennial or categorical sense except in the limited minds of positivist Orientalists and their domestic native informers; biographies mirror the fears and desires, hopes and aspirations of those who write them. Had it not been for the biographies of the prophet of Islam written by Ibn Ishaq (died 768 CE) and Ibn Hisham (died 834 CE) or for the monumental historical work of al-Tabari (839–923 CE) and for scores of other primary sources, how would these Orientalist friends of Ibn Warraq's write their accounts of Muhammad's life? Throughout the centuries, Muslim mystics have imagined and written one sort of life for their prophet, theologians and legal jurists others, and poets and prose stylists still others. Even the fabrication of spurious prophetic Hadiths by subsequent generations of Muslims is a healthy sign of robust cultures extrapolating from their own resources to meet the challenge of changing circumstances. And Muslims themselves have been chiefly responsible for painstakingly distinguishing the authentic and inauthentic Hadiths. By the time the two canonical collections of prophetic Hadiths by Muslim (817–875 CE) and Bukhari (810–870 CE) were put together, spurious versions and variations on these Hadiths existed for palpably political or juridical purposes. Authentic or fabricated, all Hadiths are the expressions of the inner sanctities of a people, their varied cultures, and the worldly civilization they have built.

None of these phenomena are unknown to Muslim historians and critics. The most iconoclastic and even, at times, disrespectful biographies of Muhammad and accounts of Islam have been written by Muslims themselves—Ali Dashti's Twenty-three Years being only one such. Generations of Marxist scholarship on Muhammad and Islam, written in or translated into Arabic, Persian, or Urdu, have been widely available to Muslims. Ibn Warraq fails to note that Dashti was, after all, a Muslim, as were the Syrian Sadiq al-Azm and the Sudanese Mahmud Muhammad Taha. Beginning with Ibn al-Muqaffa' (died 760 CE), there has been scarcely a period when radical and subversive thought has not been integral to Islamic intellectual history. A contemporary of Ali Dashti, Zabih Behruz, wrote a devastating satire on the theme of the Prophet's nocturnal journey, or Mi'raj. Another Iranian author, Sadeq Hedayat, wrote Toop Morvari—a hilarious (at times racist) satire on the rise of Islam. Yet another contemporary, Ahmad Kasravi, wrote persistently against Islam and the clerical class. The greatest living Iranian poet, Esma'il Khoi, living now in exile in London, continues to compose his radically anti-Islamic, anti-clerical poetry in magnificent Persian diction, with millions of Iranians inside and outside of their country reading and listening to him. Iranian, Arab, and South Asian historians have written volumes on the history of Islam from historicist, Socialist, or Marxist perspectives and generated a massive body of critical responses.

There is a whole universe of maladies in contemporary Islamic societies that need remedying. Thousands of Arab and Muslim intellectuals address them regularly, pervasively, courageously, with competence in the language of their own cultures and care for those who share their destiny. Among Muslims in Western Europe and North America, countless public intellectuals are emerging to address the rise of a whole new range of issues—from Tariq Ramadan and Tariq Modood to Abdolkarim Soroush and the late Nasr Hamid Abu Zayd. What unites them all is their concern for the people they address and aspirations for their collective destiny. Ibn Warraq, in contrast, seems to feel nothing but disgust for Muslims and their collective destiny. There are times when I believe Ibn Warraq cannot be a real human being, that he is the code name for a nightmare, a publishing gimmick, a stratagem catering to the basest common denominator of a murderous empire.

There is not a community anywhere on earth without a sense of inviolable sanctity to its collective identity, history, culture—all resting on certain iconic sets of evidence, from the Hebrew Bible to the American Constitution. It is that sanctity, integral to a people's sense of dignity, that Ibn Warraq wants to steal from Muslims—thus preparing them to become what Giorgio Agamben calls homo sacer, "naked life", so that when they are massacred in multitudes, not event the dignity of the word "Palestinians" will be attached to their slaughtered numbers.

FLUSHING THE QURAN DOWN THE TOILET

Having discovered the historical Muhammad in 2000, in 2002 Ibn Warraq went on to tell his readers about what the Quran really says in a book by that title. He spends the Introduction trying to disguise the fact that he does not know Arabic. "Muslims in general," he writes, "have a tendency to disarm any criticisms of Islam and in particular the Koran by asking if the critic has read the Koran in the original Arabic ... "[39] He complains of their "almost mystical and rather irrational attitude to the untranslatability of the Koran." (There are Muslims who have the same attitude toward Hamlet and the Bhagavad-Gita.) Hiding behind the irrelevant fact that for the majority of Muslims Arabic is the liturgical language of their faith (as Latin has been for Christians and Hebrew for Jews—who often do not speak it) rather than the functional language of their quotidian and literary lives, Ibn Warraq proceeds to deliver a phantasmagoric account of the "Afro-Asiatic, Semitic, Aramaic, Syriac, and Arabic" division of languages—only to hide his ignorance of Arabic, which is particularly embarrassing for someone publishing a book on *What the Koran Really Says*—not merely says, or nearly says, but really says.

The substance of the book is, again, a collection of old and new Orientalist scholarship, this time on the text of the Quran—facts, observations, and speculations long known to the scholarly communities, here resuscitated and renarrated in a language and diction that tries to demonstrate that Muslims themselves have failed to understand their own sacred text critically.

But readers of Ibn Warraq should actually be told that every single letter—every consonant and every vowel—of the Quran has been the subject of libraries and then more libraries of the most meticulous exegetical and hermeneutic scrutiny for more than 1400 years, beginning centuries before the predatory European colonialism manufactured its intelligence arm and called it Orientalism. More than 500 years before Christopher Columbus stumbled on this continent and commenced the genocide of its native inhabitants, Abu Ja'far Muhammad Ibn Jarir al-Tabari (839–923 CE) composed his *Jami' al-Bayan fi Tafsir al-Qur'an* (*A Complete Compendium on the Interpretation of the Quran*); by then the vast body of Quranic exegesis in Arabic was already so massive that al-Tabari had to sift through libraries of commentary to provide a succinct summary of various linguistic, juridical, theological, and philosophical interpretations. Since al-Tabari, they have only multiplied. It was not until the beginning of the nineteenth century that Orientalism began delivering its mercenary services to colonialism in earnest. By then Muslim scholars had left not a single fat'ha in their sacred text unturned. We are nowhere near even articulating the hermeneutic spectrum of their speculative reflections. The catastrophe of academic scholasticism and the privatization of scholarly minds is that the public space has been left vacant for voices like Ibn Warraq's to determine the nature of public discourse in matters of vital importance. There is very little distance between *The Wall Street Journal*'s giving Ibn Warraq space to denigrate Muslims and their sacred text and that very text's being flushed down the toilet by the US military personnel as a way of tormenting Muslim inmates in their custody.[40] As Kanaan Makiya and Fouad Ajami's pronounce-ments prepared the US population for the US-led invasion of Iraq, and as Lynndie England and Azar Nafisi represented the two sides of the same coin tossed in Abu Ghraib, Ibn Warraq paved the way in 2002 for what American military torturers have done ever since in Guantanamo Bay.

THE CASE AGAINST ISLAM

I have read Ibn Warraq first and foremost as an act of penance for my academic share in having contributed to a secluded scholarly language and discourse about Islam that has made that entire body of scholarship irrelevant to the public domain—leaving the space open for charlatans like Ibn Warraq to spread their venom. I have also read him to see just what nonsense is it that he is feeding his readers. If none of my academic colleagues take him seriously enough to waste their time on him, I do not blame them. But in the manner that old-fashioned anthropologists went into the jungles to learn about what they called "primitive lives", I have had to make my own journey to see how the native informers spread misinforma-tion about and hatred towards millions of human beings. But I am almost done with my diagnosis of this particularly case.

The subject of Ibn Warraq's most recent banality is apostasy.[41] *Leaving Islam* (2003) begins with a long exposé of what Ibn Warraq calls the "theory and practice of apostasy in Islam". After giving an incomplete and fallacious account of the juridical position of various schools of Islamic law on the issue, he reports on the recent cases of Nawal al-Saadawi, the late Nasr Hamid Abu Zayd, and Mahmud Muhammad Taha—three public intellectuals, two Egyptian and a Sudanese, who in one way or another angered the juridical establishment of their respective countries. None of the three can be said to have abandoned their faith. All three wrote in Arabic and published under their own names. Ibn Warraq, of course, cannot read them in Arabic—nor can he read al-Rawandi or Abu al-Ala' al-Ma'arri, who also wrote in Arabic, nor Omar Khayyam, Sadeq Hedayat, and Ali Dashti, who wrote in Persian.

Toward the end of the last book, Ibn Warraq adds something new. Apparently he and his sponsors have created a website and encouraged people to send in emails with ugly stories about Islam; he has collected these emails and published them in this section. Every single one of these accounts is anonymous, and thus it is impossible to verify even whether real people wrote them. The same is true of a collection of essays written by putative Muslims, both natives and converts and all with fictitious names, who have written Ibn Warraq about abandoning their faith; some representative titles are "Why I Left Islam: My Passage From Faith to Enlightenment", "A Journal of my Escape from the Hell of Islam", "Islamic Terrorism and the Genocide in Bangladesh", "An Iranian Girlhood and Islamic Barbarism", "Floods, Droughts, Islam, and other Natural Calamities", "Liberation from Muhammadan Ideology", "My Malaise", and "A Nightmare in Tunisia". As for the substance of these writings, here is Ali Sina from Iran: "Muslims honestly believe that the great Western civilization has its roots in Islam."[42] Sheraz Malik from Pakistan: "When I came to the United States, I saw other nationalities and ethnic groups close up; nice Hindus, white people, Mexicans, Christians, Chinese, Buddhists, Indonesians, and so on. It is not possible that these nice people can burn in hell eternally. Take Mother Teresa or Princess Diana, for example. It is not possible for these nice women who had nice hearts to burn in fire forever. Muslims don't think about this. They take the burning in fire very lightly. Burn your little finger today, just the tip of it, and see how painful it is."[43] Abul Kasem from Bangladesh: "Islam thrives because of oil prices. Once the world finds alternative sources of energy and the price of oil falls to $1.00 a barrel, Islam will surely die. Till then the world has to go through this Islamic madness."[44]

In the concluding pages of *Leaving Islam*, Ibn Warraq once again turns to the embarrassing fact that he does not know Arabic. But note how fraudulently he operates:

> It is quite common in this context to hear two arguments from Muslims and apologists of Islam: the language argument, and that old standby of crooked, lying politicians: "you have quoted out of context." Let us look at the language argument first. You are asked aggressively, "Do you know Arabic?" Then you are told triumphantly, "You have to read it in the original Arabic to understand it fully." Western freethinkers and atheists are usually reduced to sullen silence with these Muslim tactics; they indeed become rather coy and self-defensive when it comes to criticism of Islam, feebly complaining, "Who am I to criticize Islam? I do not know any Arabic."[45]

Ibn Warraq begs to differ: "You do not need to know Arabic to criticize Islam or the Koran ... Paul Kurts does not know Arabic but he did a great job on Islam in his book *The Transcendental Temptation.*[46]

His last act of treachery is to give his readers the addresses of no less than 114 websites devoted to hostile and racist attacks on Islam, plus numerous books he deems harmful to Muslims. Of the 114 addresses he gives (is that one for each chapter of the Quran?), 29 have been set up by Christian fundamentalists; 13 belong to anti-Muslim Hindu nationalists; eight belong to anti-Palestinian right-wing Zionists; and the rest are equally hostile to Islam and Muslims. From such an assortment of websites this champion of reason and historical truth wishes his readers to achieve a scholarly understanding of Islam.

An Iraqi detainee in Abu Ghraib named Amin Said al-Sheikh was asked by a US soldier who was torturing him whether he believed in anything. He replied, "I believe in Allah." "But I believe in torture," the liberator of Iraq responded, "and I will torture you." Another US soldier, meanwhile, struck his broken leg and ordered him to curse Islam. "Because they started to hit my broken leg," al-Sheikh reported, "I curse my religion. They ordered me to thank Jesus I'm alive."[47] To me, both the American torturers are morally superior to Ibn Warraq—because Ibn Warraq, here in the United States, gave those monsters the ammunition to perpetrate the crimes they committed at Abu Ghraib.

Let me conclude—and, I hope, cleanse my mind—with the visionary wisdom of our noble Malcolm X:

> This modern house Negro loves his master. He wants to live near him. He'll pay three times as much as the house is worth just to live near his master, and then brag about "I'm the only Negro out here." "I'm the only one on my job." "I'm the only one in this school." You're nothing but a house Negro. And if someone comes to you right now and says, "Let's separate,"you say the same thing that the house Negro said on the plantation. "What you mean, separate? From America? This good white man? Where you going to get a better job than you get here?" I mean, this is what you say. "I ain't left nothing in Africa," that's what you say. Why, you left your mind in Africa.[48]

Conclusion
Confusing the Color Line

The Jew and I: not satisfied with racializing myself, by a happy stroke of fate, I was turning more human. I was drawing closer to the Jew, my brother in misfortune.

Frantz Fanon, *Black Skin, White Masks* (1952)

So, let me place on record the following fact: the board [the Board of Deputies of British Jews] does not speak for all British Jews and certainly not for this one. Nor does the so-called Leadership Council [the Jewish Leadership Council], nor any of the organizations associated with this misbegotten event [demonstrations in support of the Israeli invasion of Gaza in 2008–09]. None of them represents me or the Judaism that I cherish and which leads me to say as follows: I condemn utterly the military offensive by the government of Israel against the people of Gaza. The loss of any human life, on whatever side of this conflict, is a terrible thing. At this juncture, though, my heart is with the Palestinians on the ground in the midst of their misery. And I extend my hand to those Israelis who are speaking out against their own government.

Brian Klug, *Guardian* (9 January 2009)

I began preparing the final draft of this book for publication just before the Mumbai attacks late in November 2008 and ended it soon after the Israeli massacre of Palestinians in Gaza commenced late in December. The first atrocity was globally condemned as the act of "Muslim terrorists", while no one ever called the latter an act of "Jewish terrorism". Those who describe the former atrocity as "Islamic terrorism" were wrong, just as they were right to refrain from calling the latter one "Jewish terrorism". One of my major arguments in this book has been that neither Islam nor Judaism, as a world religion, is responsible for any of these atrocities. What that gang of militant adventurers perpetrated in Mumbai (or, before that, in New York, London, and Madrid) was a criminal act and demanded to be denounced and prosecuted as a criminal act. The more than half-century of genocidal violence that Zionists have brought to bear against Palestinians is the latest legacy of European colonialism, and Judaism is categorically exonerated from having had anything to do with that murderous ethnic cleansing. There were scores of distinguished rabbis, like Rabbi Elmer Berger (1908–96), who opposed Zionism and its claims to any Jewish justification of the colonial enterprise in Palestine. Millions of European Jews refused to have anything to do with Zionism. European colonialism was also, and in infinitely more institutional terms, informed by Christianity—and Islam, too, has had a major presence in many empires. If Judaism, Christianity, and Islam all have a hand in colonial projects and empires, then colonialism and imperialism are predicated on an entirety different animus—economic, territorial, and military expansionism. If anything, Enlightenment modernity has been more integral to European colonialism than has any religion it sought to supplant.

Why is it, then, that the term "Islamic terrorism" is a common staple of Western European and North American journalistic, policymaking, and even scholarly parlance, but not "Jewish terrorism" (or even "Christian terrorism")? That is the issue I have sought to address in this book, in part via the instrumental category of native informers, people with brown skins and white masks and falsified consciousnesses, who I believe are significantly responsible for authenticating and corroborating this demonization of Islam and dehumanization of Muslims. A handful of demonstrators protest the ridiculing of their prophet by Danish cartoonists, and Salman Rushdie and company are up in arms with the claim that Islam is the new fascism. Israel, an entire state apparatus with a massive military machinery, massacres Palestinians by the hundreds and maims them by the thousands in Gaza, the whole world is crying out in protest—and yet Rushdie and his friends are nowhere to be seen. Rushdie, Ayaan Hirsi Ali, Fouad Ajami, Azar Nafisi, Irshad Manji, Ibn Warraq, and scores of similar self-loathing Muslims aid and abet in the visceral dehumanization of Muslims, so that when Palestinians are butchered like sheep in a slaughterhouse in full view of history (like Afghan, Iraqi, and Lebanese Muslims before them), the United States and the European Union can shrug and endorse the massacre. Look closely at the tired, frightened, angry faces of the millions of people protesting the Israeli war crimes in Western Europe and North America! Not a single one of them can you imagine reading *Reading Lolita in Tehran*.

What happened in Mumbai, I repeat, was a criminal act perpetrated by a militant band of murderous adventurers, the distant echoes of seeds that US imperialism had sown in Afghanistan and Pakistan as a way to confront the Soviet in the 1980s.[1] What has happened in Gaza is an infinitely more criminal act (by the scale of violence and the number of innocent human beings murdered, burned, maimed, and crippled) perpetrated by a genocidal colonial settlement called Israel, the last remnant of European racism in the region. Desacralizing criminal acts (and seeing them for what they are) is coterminous with decriminalizing political dissent (and celebrating it for what it inspires—resistance). What we are seeing today is exactly the opposite: criminal acts by individual Muslims are attributed to the very essence of their religion, while acts of political dissent in protest against the crimes against humanity perpetrated by the United States and Israel are criminalized. We must reverse that false and falsifying consciousness. We must be able to protest and fight back against injustice without being branded criminals, anti-Semites, terrorists; and we must be able to condemn criminal acts perpetrated by Muslims, Jews, Christians, or Hindus without implicating the faiths that hold the souls of billions of people together. But where must we start this rethink in order to find our way out of this predicament? First let us consider the full context of what we face.

RECODING RACISM IN AMERICA AND BEYOND

For eight long and murderous years (2000–08), the world was at the mercy of George W. Bush. He ruled the United States—and, with it, the world—with utter disregard for the most basic principles of human decency. He ended his term leaving a desperate and desolate world covered with human corpses and spotted with the bodies of tortured men, murdered mothers, raped women, orphaned children, ruined buildings, burned farms and burning factories, firms, and oilfields, from Afghanistan to Iraq to Palestine to Lebanon to the streets of New Orleans. There has been much talk in the United States about prosecuting Bush and his subordinates for war crimes. But no tribunal could ever issue a verdict harsh enough to equal the pain and suffering that this man caused among the poor and disenfranchised. Aided by his European and Israeli allies, and actively or passively endorsed by corrupt and incompetent Arab and Muslim heads of state, George W. Bush looks like a nightmare from which the world has finally woken up; after a clean, cold shower it may once again remember humanity, decency, and morality. Bush's last act before getting lost in historical ignominy was endorsing the Israelis' massacre of thousands of Palestinians in Gaza.

After eight catastrophic years, Americans from all walks of life, disgusted with what this man had done to the world in their name, came together on November 4, 2008, in a momentous occasion of collective redemption and catharsis, and chose Barack Hussein Obama as the first African-American to hold the highest office in the land. More profoundly, this was the expression of their highest aspirations and their hope to return to the fold of humanity and to stop embodying the principle source of menace and mayhem around the globe. But it did not take more than a mere couple of days for the euphoria of Obama's victory to begin giving way to an icy cold fear and wonder. From the windy winter cold of Chicago he announced his selection of Illinois Congressman Rahm Israel Emanuel as his chief of staff—effectively the gatekeeper of his White House. Congressman Emanuel comes from a strongly pro-Israeli family. He served in the Israeli army for a short time; his father, Benjamin Emanuel, served for a much longer period with the notorious Irgun, the Zionist terrorist organization chiefly responsible for scores of murderous acts, among them the ethnic cleansing of Palestine when Israel was being superimposed on the world map in the 1940s.[2] Throughout his presidential campaign, Obama had remained a suspicious figure to pro-Israeli voters, and no matter how hard he tried to convince them that he held the American relationship with Israel "sacrosanct", as he put it on a number of occasions, he was not completely successful. In his infamously obsequious speech in front of the American Israel Political Affairs Committee (AIPAC) soon after he declared victory in June 2008 in his pursuit of the Democratic presidential nomination, he spent a great deal of time refuting the allegations with which he had been charged—chief among them that he was a Muslim.[3] The appointment of a pro-Israeli chief of staff went a long way toward reassuring pro-Israeli lobbies and voters, and the ground opened up like an abyss under the feet of those who had hoped for something different.[4]

The disappointment that a wide spectrum of Obama supporters now faced was neither limited to this single appointment nor confined to what their candidate would do toward reconciling the idealism of his youthful community activism (over which the memory of Malcolm X shone brightly) with the pragmatism of his adult presidency vis-à-vis the predicament of Palestinians and the warmongering of the Jewish apartheid state. Every appointment that he made public in November and December 2008 called for a reassessment of his campaign promises. When he finally announced New York's junior senator, Hillary Rodham Clinton (who stands to the right of the Likud Party when it comes to Israel), as his choice for Secretary of State, and the news spread that Dennis Ross (a key AIPAC operative) would be his choice to head Middle East

Affairs, the disappointment deepened. When Israel commenced the massacre of Palestinians in Gaza late in December 2008, President-elect Obama seemed thoroughly preoccupied with the mounting economic problems that his administration was inheriting; he remained silent on the Israeli slaughter of Palestinians, calling on the mantra "We have only one president at a time". While many were dismayed, I for one was relieved that at least he did not repeat the nauseating Bush administration line that Hamas was responsible for the carnage the Israeli army was visiting upon Gaza. As we say in Persian: Ma ra beh kheyr-e to ommid nist, shar marasan. We have no hope in your doing any good; prithee do us no evil.

It did not help matters when Rahm Emanuel's father, Benjamin Emanuel, gave an interview to the Israeli newspaper *Ma'ariv* in which he predicted that "obviously" his son "will influence the president to be pro-Israel. Why wouldn't he be? What is he, an Arab? He's not going to clean the floors of the White House."[5] The crudely racist remark delighted Zionists from Tel Aviv to New York and created havoc among the Arab and Muslim communities in the US, forcing the American-Arab Anti-Discrimination Committee (ADC)—hardly known for its daring imagination or principled positions on anything—to write a letter to Rahm Emanuel demanding that he repudiate his father's comment and send a copy to the president-elect. According to reports, the younger Emanuel called Mary Rose Oaker, the ADC president, to dissociate himself from his father's remark and apologize.[6]

Under ordinary circumstances this apology would have been the end of the matter. But these are not ordinary times. The unabated and in fact growing racism toward Muslims in general and Arabs in particular in North America (and Western Europe) requires far more serious attention—for it is the newest gestation of classical Christian anti-Semitism and white supremacist racism, now coming together in their fullest unfolding. For what seems to have happened since the events of 9/11, but particularly during the presidential election of 2008, is the semiotic transmutation of "blacks" and "Jews" into "Arabs" and "Muslims", respectively, in the evolving lexicon of American racism—and for this reason Benjamin Emanuel's remark deserves closer attention, as does the entire presidential election in 2008, during which, on countless occasions, this recodification of American racism was fully on display, particularly when it came to the figure and phenomenon of Barack Hussein Obama himself.

What does it mean, exactly, to say: "He's not going to clean the floors of the White House"—of all things? What does it signify?

Who has stereotypically, and in a racist cliché, cleaned the floors of the White House? Certainly not Arabs—though perhaps in Israel, where cheap Palestinian labor is systematically abused, Israelis are used to seeing Arabs clean their floors. In Washington DC and the rest of the United States, and certainly in the White House, a whole history of African slavery has determined who, as a matter of racist cliché, cleans the floors. In the racist mind of the aging Benjamin Emanuel—who does not know the language of concealing one's bigotry and speaks like the Irgun terrorist that he was—he simply switches the African for the Arab and lets go of "the values upon which he has raised his family". What the senior Emanuel uttered is not all that odd for an Israeli racist. The domain of anti-Arab bigotry in Israel, from which Benjamin Emanuel draws freely, is not limited to Irgun terrorists. "Mohammad's a pig", and "Death to Arabs" are the staples of Israeli racism regularly sprayed on mosques and spewed at the residents of occupied Palestine, as is the hurling of severed pigs' heads into Muslim houses of worship.[7] What is embedded in the senior Emanuel's remark is the regenerative transfusion of two differently coded modes of racism: Ashkenazi Israeli racism toward Arabs (and, for that matter, Sephardic Jews) and white American racism toward blacks. In a simple act of cross-codification, the two modes of racism come together and announce not just a mere Israelification of American political culture but also the transformation of racist registers of Blacks into Arabs (or "sand niggers" as they have been popularly dubbed).

This sort of racism, of course, was by no means limited to Obama's camp. Arabs and Muslims fared no better during the beleaguered campaign of Senator John McCain. Capably aided by his longtime friend and confident Senator Joe Lieberman of Connecticut, who in American politics acts as though he were an Israeli agent at large,[8] Senator McCain offered his principle take on Arabs and Muslims throughout his campaign in a very simple mantra: "Radical Islamic extremism is the transcendent challenge of the twenty-first century."[9] In particular his supporters afforded central significance to Barack Hussein Obama's middle name, explicitly or implicitly identifying him as an Arab or a Muslim at a time when the signifier "Hussein" was a Pavlovian signal for Saddam Hussein, the deposed and executed president of Iraq.

An exemplary instance occurred on February 26, 2008, in Cincinnati, Ohio, when a conservative radio talk show host named Bill Cunningham repeatedly and mockingly intoned Barack Hussein Obama's full name, with exaggerated emphasis on his middle name, before inviting McCain to the podium. The incident was echoed during many other Republican campaign rallies, both when McCain was being introduced and when his vice-presidential nominee, Governor Sarah Palin of Alaska, was asked to the podium. In the end even Obama made fun of his middle name, at the Alfred E. Smith Memorial Foundation Dinner in New York on October 16, 2008: "Who is Barack Obama?" he asked, tongue in cheek, mocking a Republican refrain against him. "Contrary to the rumors you have heard, I was not born in a manger. I was actually born on Krypton and sent here by my father, Jor-El, to save the planet Earth. Many of you ... know that I got my name, Barack, from my father. What you may not know is that Barack is actually Swahili for 'that one' (a reference to an awkward moment in a previous debate when McCain had referred to Obama as 'that one'). And I got my middle name from somebody who obviously didn't think I'd ever run for President ... Anyway, that's who I really am. But in the spirit of full disclosure, there are a few October surprises you'll be finding out about in the coming weeks. First of all, my middle name is not what you think. It's actually Steve. That's right. Barack Steve Obama."[10]

THE ENEMY WITHIN

The McCain campaign's emphasis on Obama's middle name was a way of making him seem foreign and thus dangerous, strange and untrustworthy. (The name is, of course, both Arabic and Islamic, the most famous Hussein being the Prophet's grandson and the second Shi'i Imam, Imam Hussein ibn Ali [626–680 CE].)

Another infamous campaign scene took place in Lakeville, Minnesota on October 10, 2008. A white Republican volunteer named Gayle Quinnell stood up in the middle of a rally and told Senator McCain, "I don't trust Obama. I have read about him and he is an Arab"; to which Senator McCain responded, "No ma'am, no ma'am. He's a decent family man, a citizen that I just happen to have disagreements with on fundamental issues. That's what this campaign is all about. He's not, thank you." Note that in McCain's response being an Arab disqualifies one from being "a decent family man", and that his anti-immigration anxieties surface in his identifying Obama as a "citizen" and thus categorizing Arabs as "alien"—even if they were born and raised in America. But far more significant are the staccato pauses in between Gayle Quinnell's phrases, as she tries to conceal her racism and joggles and shifts in her hesitant diction: "He's not," she first says, but does not complete her sentence. Then she continues, "He's a ... " and again hesitates. Then she spurts it out: "He is an Arab."[11] The pause after the first "He's not" might have meant (for example) "He's not an American." The one after "He's a ... " could have been for what Obama is—an African-American. The history of American racism and its shifting registers pulsates in those hesitant, stuttering moments before she finally says, "He is an Arab."

Between the statements of Gayle Quinnell—a white American woman—in early October and Benjamin Emanuel—an Ashkenazi Israeli man—in early November, one made just before and one just after Obama was elected, we see the transmutation of "black" into "Arab" that was already under way in the preceding months. The black had now become the Arab while, at the same time, the Jew was busy becoming the Muslim.

Obama's identification as an Arab was paralleled by his simultaneous identification as a Muslim (in the accusatory tone used for the Jew in classical Christian anti-Semitic parlance). Obama's father was an African Muslim, his mother an American Christian. In the course of his life, as had become more publicly evident, Obama had opted to identify with his father's race but not his religion, and with his mother's faith but not her race. This not uncommon cherry-picking in identity formation is predicated on the checkered psychological disposition that underlies Obama's social persona— who he is and who he has willed himself to become.[12] He entered the American political arena as a black man and as a Christian. But that a Black Muslim, Louis Farrakhan, had endorsed him for the presidency soon assumed a particularly pointed edge, when in the course of a primary presidential debate with Senator Hillary Clinton in Ohio, on February 26, 2008, the late American journalist Tim Russert of NBC asked Obama point blank whether he denounced Louis Farrakhan's endorsement. As an opinion piece written by Richard Cohen of *The Washington Post* had argued more than a month earlier, Obama's problem with Farrakhan's endorsement dated back to 2007, when the church of which he was a member, Trinity United Baptist Church of Christ, presided over by Reverend Jeremiah Wright, had given its Dr. Jeremiah A. Wright Jr. Trumpeter Award to Louis Farrakhan; Cohen took exception to the award and saw in Obama's attitude toward it a test of his loyalty to the Zionist cause.[13] In the course of the February Ohio debate, however, Obama was forced, by both Russert and Hillary Clinton, to "repudiate and denounce" Farrakhan. The incident left Obama, as he distanced himself from a man of his estranged father's race and faith, a Black Muslim, more at ease not identifying with either; put another way, as both his liberal and conservative supporters began to posit, his politics were now decidedly "post-racial". His politics were no such thing. Rather, racism in the United States was being recodified right in front of our eyes.

At the very moment Obama was busy denying "accusations" of being a Muslim and embracing his Christianity while positing a fake post-racial politics, in March 2008, as ironic fate would have it, the same Reverend Jeremiah Wright, a prophetic liberation theologian of extraordinary passion and conviction, popped up from the heart of Obama's Christianity and forced him to dodge yet again. He dodged in April, by trying to contextualize Reverend Wright's decidedly anti-racist, anti-apartheid, and anti-colonial remarks in a way that would make them palatable to white liberals. When that failed and Reverend Wright would not be silenced, he dodged again in May by altogether denouncing his long time pastor and leaving his church.[14] It was remarkable if scarcely noted that between March and May 2008 Islamic and Christian liberation theologies came to the fore: by now, anti-Islamic sentiment in the United States was so rampant that few were aware of the irony when, in the act of disowning Islam and allowing it to be demonized, Obama found himself clasped to the bosom of a revolutionary Christian liberation theologian whom the white Christian Zionists that Obama believed (wrongly) he needed on his side in order to win the election found equally frightening. Since Wright's church had just celebrated Louis Farrakhan, it is fair to say that Islamic liberation theology was never more revolutionary than in Jeremiah Wright's Christianity.[15]

During the long and tiring summer of 2008, as Obama and Clinton battled each other in state after state, the "accusations" continued—that Obama was a Muslim, that if elected he would take the oath of office on the Quran rather than the Bible, that he had attended a madrasa in Indonesia, where his mother had lived with her second Muslim husband. (Obama never dared or cared to state publicly that while he was not a Muslim there was nothing wrong with being a Muslim.[16]) These flaky accusations pale, however, next to the *New York Times*' attempt to brand Obama as a Muslim. At a crucial moment in the campaign, when Hillary Clinton, whom the *Times* had endorsed, was battling relentlessly but ever more hopelessly, the Newspaper of the Record suggested that not only was Obama a Muslim but he was, in fact, irreversibly so.

On May 12, 2008, an Op-Ed piece by Edward N. Luttwak argued that Obama was indubitably a Muslim because he had been born to a Muslim father, and according to Islam (Luttwak believed), when you are born a Muslim you are a Muslim always, and you dare abandon the faith on the sure punishment of death. Obama was a charismatic figure, Luttwak agreed, and his charisma, he feared, might make him popular with Muslims around the world.

> But it is a mistake to conflate his African identity with his Muslim heritage. Senator Obama is half African by birth and Africans can understandably identify with him. In Islam, however, there is no such thing as a half-Muslim. Like all monotheistic religions, Islam is an exclusive faith. As the son of the Muslim father, Senator Obama was born a Muslim under Muslim law as it is universally understood. It makes no difference that, as Senator Obama has written, his father said he renounced his religion. Likewise, under Muslim law based on the Koran his mother's Christian background is irrelevant. [17]

Luttwak was arguing not only that Obama was a Muslim (which at this crucial time in the primaries was like a kiss of death) but also that, by virtue of his having declared that he had left his religion, Muslims were legally bound to kill him. He made no mention of Senator Robert Kennedy or his demented assassin, Sirhan Bishara Sirhan, but the implicit reference was quite evident. Not long after Luttwak's piece appeared, Senator Clinton, in a meeting with the editorial board of South Dakota's Sioux Falls Argus-Leader on May 23, 2003, defended her staying the course against the odds by saying, "My husband did not wrap up the nomination in 1992 until he won the California primary somewhere in the middle of June, right? We all remember Bobby Kennedy was assassinated in June in California."[18] Here, the widely criticized death-wish for Obama cross-checked with Luttwak's implicit suggestion that a Muslim might kill him. Muslims, after all, are murderous assassins—and one of them (the Judeo-Christian God forbid) might very well be in the White House come January.

Luttwak continued:

> His conversion, however, was a crime in Muslim eyes; it is "irtidad" or "ridda", usually translated from the Arabic as "apostasy", but with connotations of rebellion and treason. Indeed, it is the worst of all crimes that a Muslim can commit, worse than murder.

Luttwak then launched into a juridical discussion of how the apostate ought to be killed:

> With few exceptions, the jurists of all Sunni and Shiite schools prescribe execution for all adults who leave the faith not under duress; the recommended punishment is beheading at the hands of a cleric, although in recent years there have been both stonings and hangings.

At this point, perhaps realizing he had gone too far in his fantasies, he back-pedaled a bit:

> Because no government is likely to allow the prosecution of a President Obama—not even those of Iran and Saudi Arabia, the only two countries where Islamic religious courts dominate over secular law—another provision of Muslim law is perhaps more relevant: it prohibits punishment for any Muslim who kills any apostate, and effectively prohibits interference with such a killing. At the very least, that would complicate the security planning of state visits by President Obama to Muslim countries, because the very act of protecting him would be sinful for Islamic security guards. More broadly, most citizens of the Islamic world would be horrified by the fact of Senator Obama's conversion to Christianity once it became widely known—as it would, no doubt, should he win the White House. This would compromise the ability of governments in Muslim nations to cooperate with the United States in the fight against terrorism, as well as American efforts to export democracy and human rights abroad.[19]

The moral of this spooky campfire story was (1) we must not elect this man—he is a Muslim after all; and (2) should he be elected anyway, he must never set foot in a Muslim country or he will be killed with legal impunity. Was this an attempt to poison any potential rapprochement with the Islamic world before Obama could even begin to implement it? Luttwak addressed that subject, too:

> That an Obama presidency would cause such complications in our dealings with the Islamic world is not likely to be a major factor with American voters, and the implication is not that it should be. But of all the well-meaning desires projected on Senator Obama, the hope that he would decisively improve relations with the world's Muslims is the least realistic.

Realism, in his opinion, was, first, to make sure Americans knew that Obama was legally a Muslim, whatever his claims to the contrary (this at a time when his campaign was actively distancing him not just from Muslims but even from his identity as a black candidate) and, second, to make sure that no Muslim should be deluded that he might bring a fairer approach to the issue of Palestine, the central concern of more than 1.5 billion Muslims around the world. As far as Luttwak's qualifications to offer this jurisprudential dispensation on Islamic law, the *Times* had only this to say: "Edward N. Luttwak, a fellow at the Center for Strategic and International Studies, is the author of "Strategy: The Logic of War and Peace."[20]

A couple of weeks later, on June 1, 2008, the *Times*, deciding, perhaps, that Luttwak's Op-Ed piece had been anti-Obama, anti-Muslim, and altogether Islamophobic to an unprecedented and scandalous degree, published a piece by its public editor, Clark Hoyt ("Entitled to Their Opinions, Yes. But Their Facts?"), in which Hoyt did his best to rectify the situation by giving space to reasonable voices that questioned the paper's wisdom in publishing Luttwak.[21] From Hoyt we learn that Luttwak is actually a military historian, not a scholar of Islamic law. Hoyt caught Luttwak out on his fabrications, innuendos, and insinuations, particularly on the point that a state visit to a Muslim country would present security challenges "because the very act of protecting him would be sinful for Islamic security guards".

"At a time when fears about Obama's security keep bubbling to the surface and an online whispering campaign suggests that he is secretly a Muslim," Hoyt noted, " ... the Luttwak thesis was a double whammy: Obama cannot escape his Muslim history, and a lot of Muslims might want to kill him for trying." He further emphasized that "Op-Ed writers are entitled to emphasize facts that support their arguments and minimize others that do not. But they are not entitled to get the facts wrong or to so mangle them so that they present a false picture."

Hoyt's judgment: "I interviewed five Islamic scholars, at five American universities, recommended by a variety of sources as experts in the field. All of them said that Luttwak's interpretation of Islamic law was wrong." He then took the Op-Ed editors to task and concluded,

All the scholars argued that Luttwak had a rigid, simplistic view of Islam that failed to take into account its many strains and the subtleties of its religious law, which is separate from the secular laws in almost all Islamic nations. The Islamic press and television have reported extensively on the United States presidential election, they said, and Obama's Muslim roots and his Christian religion are well known, yet there have been no suggestions in the Islamic world that he is an apostate.

Luttwak was unrepentant and accused the scholars Hoyt had consulted of portraying Islam as "a tolerant religion of peace" when, in his opinion, it was "intolerant". As for the *Times* itself:

[David] Shipley, the Op-Ed editor, said he regretted not urging Luttwak to soften his language about possible assassination, given how sensitive the subject is. But he said he did not think the Op-Ed page was under any obligation to present an alternative view, beyond some letters to the editor.

Clark responded:

I do not agree. With a subject this charged, readers would have been far better served with more than a single, extreme point of view. When writers purport to educate readers about complex matters, and they are arguably wrong, I think the *Times* cannot label it opinion and let it go at that.

The Republican campaign scene that made Obama an Arab (standing for black) and the *New York Times* piece that made him a Muslim (standing for a Jew) then came together on a now-famous *New Yorker* cover (drawn by Barry Blitt for the July 21, 2008, issue of the magazine) of Barack and Michelle Obama.[22] Whether in jest or not (the cover did offend the Obama camp), it was the pictorial summation of everything that was fearful about the Obamas to white Americans.

Hanging from the wall of the Oval Office behind Obama is a portrait of Osama bin Laden. Burning in a fireplace underneath it is an American flag. Obama sports a shalwar kameez, a turban, and a pair of sandals, while Michelle Obama totes a gun and a round of ammunition, wears an Afro that recalls the Angela Davis of the 1960s, and features guerrilla-style military fatigues. The couple, fist-bumping in a gesture of solidarity and success, are black/Muslim/Arab, and they are in the White House—of all the colors that a house might have.

The identification of Obama with Arabs, Muslims, and thus ipso facto with terrorists had started much earlier in the American media. The most glaring early example occurred as far back as January 2007, when CNN broadcast a picture of Osama bin Laden in an advertisement for a feature the network was running about him and captioned it, "Where's Obama?" After an outcry, CNN's Wolf Blitzer reported that he had "personally" called Obama to apologize for the mistake; a campaign aide said Obama accepted the apology and believed the incident had been a mistake—even though the letter "B" and the letter "S" lie quite a distance apart on American keyboards.[23]

The prominence of Obama's middle name as a signifier of his Arab/Muslim identity would not leave him until the last days of the presidential campaign, if ever—he declared that he intended to be sworn in with his full name, Barack Hussein Obama.[24] At one point even his style of dress was compared with Iranian president Mahmoud Ahmadinejad's. His patriotism was questioned when it was pointed out that he did not wear a lapel pin of the American flag—for which he overcompensated at the speech he gave before AIPAC soon after he won the Democratic presidential nomination by wearing a pin with double flags of the United States and Israel. During one of his last campaign stops, at a Florida synagogue, one man said that if he "changed his name to Barry, I would vote for him". Barry was a name he used to go by, Obama responded, adding that his name was similar to the Hebrew name Baruch—"It means one who's blessed."[25] The closer the country got to Election Day, the more charges were raised against him—that he was a "socialist", because of his economic programs and taxation policies; that he "palled around" with terrorists, because he knew the former Weatherman Bill Ayers, because he had Palestinian friends, because in Chicago he had known Rashid Khalidi and had met with Edward Said.

The irony of all this lies in the hidden paradox that the more his adversaries tried to paint him into an Arab/Muslim corner, and the more he tried to distance himself from it and practice a post-racial politics, the more he called upon the rhetorical devices of black orators, among them the greatest Black Muslim America has ever known: Malcolm X himself. In a piece in the *Washington Post* just before Obama's inauguration, Michael Eric Dyson gave a panoramic view of the various ways in which Obama had incorporated patterns of "black speech, whose best rhetoricians marry style and substance to spawn a uniquely earthy eloquence". In a key comparison, Dyson noted how in a crucial speech, on January 23, 2008, in Sumter, South Carolina, Obama,

> addressing a largely African American audience … let loose with the black tradition known as signifying—in which the speaker hints at ideas or meanings that are veiled to outsiders. "They're trying to bamboozle you," he said. "It's the same old okie-doke. Y'all know about okie doke, right?" he asked, as the audience erupted in laughter at his comic timing. Keeping up the humor, he protested the idea that he was a Muslim, insisting, in a spurt of black English, that "I've been a member of the same church for almost 20 years, prayin' to Jesus—wit' my Bible." And he repeated his theme of political trickery: "They try to bamboozle you. Hoodwink ya. Try to hoodwink ya. All right, I'm having too much fun here."[26]

Taking this last set of phrases, Tyson then rightly noted,

> ironically, in style and substance, Obama's flight of rhetoric echoed, of all people, Malcolm X—or at least the one portrayed in Spike Lee's biopic, who says in a memorable speech from the film, "You've been hoodwinked. You've been had. You've been took. You've been led astray, led amok. You've been bamboozled." Obama was making a risky move that played to inside-group understanding even as he campaigned in the white mainstream: While denying that he was Muslim, he fastened onto the rhetoric of the most revered Black Muslim, mimicking his tone and rhythm beat for beat.[27]

There were innumerable positive aspects to Obama's presidential campaign in inter-racial and inter-gender relations, as there have been afterward. The Obama-Emanuel pairing (as president and White House chief of staff) addressed the longstanding anger and hostility between the African-American and Jewish communities and could potentially go a long way toward alleviating it. The Obama-Clinton pairing (as president and secretary of state) did the same for the African-American and white women voters who were at times bitterly divided during the presidential campaign over the two figures. But they came at a cost to two recently constituted pariahs, on which all these actors concurred: the vilification of Arabs and Muslims.

DEPOLITICIZING THE CRIMINAL/DECRIMINALIZING THE POLITICAL

The recodification of racism in North America whereby the Jew became the Muslim and the black the brown (or Arab, in a color-coded register) was predicated on a fundamental logical flaw, whereby the criminal acts of a band of militant Muslim adventurers was politicized, identified as definitive to a world religion, and called "Islamic terrorism". Islam is a world religion; terrorism is a political act, indiscriminately targeting civilian populations—examples of which in modern history include the Irgun in Palestine, the Khmer Rouge in Cambodia, the Janjaweed in Darfur. The events of 9/11 and other similar incidents are sporadic criminal acts—conditioned, of course, by wanton American imperialism around the globe—and entirely divorced from any purposeful political project.

The nonsense that American media experts have handed out about "Jihadism" is entirely fallacious. The period when Islam was integral to national liberation movements ended with the Iranian revolution of 1979; it is now emerging once again in Palestine's Hamas, Lebanon's Hezbollah, and Iraq's Mahdi's Army, movements that are categorically different from the militant adventurism of Osama bin Laden and al-Qaeda.[28] The aggressive politicization of the criminal acts of militant Muslims (by their neoconservative American counterparts) was inevitably accompanied by the criminalization of legitimate political acts—so that national liberation movements like Hamas, Hezbollah, and Mahdi's Army have been ipso facto criminalized. In other words, the criminal acts of Osama bin Laden and his followers were politicized so that the political projects of Hamas, Hezbollah, and Mahdi's Army could be criminalized—and that is the principal distortion that needs to be corrected.

The first step in confronting the recodification of racism in the United States, and through it racism in general, is to begin divorcing criminal acts from Islam—or any other religion, for that matter—and the best example of how this can be done comes from the financial world. Amidst the financial meltdown of Wall Street in late 2008 came news of a towering investment veteran named Bernard L. Madoff who had put together a $50 billion Ponzi scheme that swindled far and wide, erasing the life savings of many individuals and the endowments of many institutions. That Madoff was Jewish, as were some of his major clients, prompted an ABC News report, "Madoff Case Sparks Anti-Semitism Fears."[29] "Of all the words that had been used to describe the Bernard L. Madoff scandal," according to the report:

> the most emotionally charged may be "Jewish". The disgraced investment guru is accused of orchestrating a $50 billion Ponzi scheme that preyed heavily on fellow Jews and ultimately drained the fortunes of numerous Jewish charities and institutions ... the allegations against Madoff are particularly wrenching for some in the Jewish community, who fear that the sensational case is fanning vicious stereotypes about Jews that go back to the Middle Ages. The Anti-Defamation League cites a spike in anti-Semitic comments online after Madoff's Dec. 11 arrest. A columnist for the Israeli newspaper *Ha'aretz* lamented the case as "the answer to every Jew-hater's wish list". And the American Jewish Committee's executive director, David A. Harris, wrote a letter to the *New York Times* criticizing what he saw as "a striking emphasis" on Madoff's faith in one of the paper's many stories about the scandal. The case is "fodder for the bigots", Abraham H. Foxman, the ADL's national director, said in an interview this week with The Associated Press. "It's both embarrassing and it's painful."

All those who have objected to the implication that Madoff's being a Jew had anything to do with his criminal behavior were correct. There are scores of unscrupulous investors in the United States and around the world, and corruption is an equal-opportunity employer. But why, then, cannot precisely the same logical argument be applied to "Muslim terrorists"? Did Madoff do what he did because he was a Jew or because he was a swindler? Obviously the latter. Then why cannot Mohammad Atta, Mullah Omar, and Osama bin Laden be seen for the psychopaths and sociopaths they are? Why cannot it be recognized that they committed their criminal acts because they are criminals and not because they are Muslims? The ABC report continues:

> It's difficult to describe the [Madoff] case in any detail without mentioning Madoff's religion. The 70-year-old money manager and former Nasdaq stock market chairman donated hundreds of thousands of dollars a year, much of it to Jewish causes. And many of the known victims of his business, Bernard L. Madoff Investment Securities, are big names in Jewish life. Yeshiva University, one of the nation's foremost Jewish institutions of

higher education, lost $110 million; Hadassah, the Women's Zionist Organization of America, lost $90 million; director Steven Spielberg's Wunderkinder Foundation acknowledged unspecified losses; and a $15 million foundation established by Holocaust survivor and writer Elie Wiesel was wiped out. Jewish federations and hospitals have lost millions and some foundations have had to close.[30]

Neither Osama bin Laden nor Mullah Omar is nearly so well-grounded in any Muslim community. They are militant vagabonds with no organic link to any Muslim society. Madoff's deep-rooted connection to Jewish causes and communities does not implicate Judaism or Jews as such in any of his criminal acts, for as the ABC report immediately adds:

> The Baptist Foundation of Arizona told investors their money would build churches while paying returns. In fact, their savings were sucked into what authorities called a $550 million Ponzi scheme in the 1980s and 1990s. Several foundation officials were sentenced to prison in 2006 and 2007. Chicago real estate investment firm Sunrise Equities Inc. had the blessing of Muslim clerics, who said its dividends conformed with Islamic laws against earning interest. Its owner disappeared this past August, leaving 200 of his fellow Muslim immigrants with losses that could total $50 million.[31]

If militant criminals can be Jews (Baruch Goldstein), Christians (Seung-Hui Cho), or Muslims (Muhammad Atta), then their religion is entirely irrelevant to their criminality, and their criminality does not have any bearing on their religion or their religious communities. The ABC report concludes with a crucial point:

> In his letter to the *Times* about a Madoff article, the ABC's Harris wrote: "Yes, he is Jewish. We get it. But was this relevant to his being arrested for cheating investors, or so key to his evolution as a businessman that it needed to be hammered home again and again?" The Rabbinical Council of America issued a statement Wednesday underscoring that "there is no reason to believe such terrible behavior is more common among Jews" than anyone else.[32]

Harris could not be more correct. May we, then, extend his perfectly logical point and say, "Yes, Osama bin Laden is Muslim. We get it.

But was this relevant to his being a militant adventurer, or so key to his evolution as a violent vagabond that it needed to be hammered home again and again?" Or, as the Rabbinical Council of America might say, there is no reason to believe such terrible behavior is more common among Muslims.

BROWN SKIN, WHITE MASKS, FALSE CONSCIOUSNESS

The decodification of racism and the depoliticization of criminal acts, as a prelude to the decriminalization of legitimate political movements, will have to be predicated on a direct understanding of the semiotic underpinning of a virtual empire—the American empire as a metanarrative that persists and thrives on signifying itself with extended guns and shortened memories of its place in the world. The central function of native informers is to sustain the mirage of this virtual empire. Neither that virtual empire, nor the function of native informers in sustaining its delusion, nor indeed the recodification of racism should be fetishized, for they are all predicated on a false consciousness, a self-alienation, that has meta-phorically over-extended itself and now narratively metastasized. The most significant lesson in the current recodification of racism in America is that racism as a phenomenon stays constant while its signifiers change visual and affective registers—from black to brown, from Jew to Muslim, at the center of which bifurcations remains a fictive white Christian interlocutor who demands and exacts racialized superiority. Islam is the new Judaism, Muslims the new Jews, Islamophobia the new anti-Semitism, and brown the new black—all in the racialized imagination of a white-identified supremacy that must first alienate (both in itself and of itself) in order to rule.

My categorization of the figure of the native informers in this book marks a particular moment in the making and breaking of the virtual empire they serve and under whose shadow humanity at large lives perilously. This empire thrives on the stories it tells itself about liberty and democracy, or about "the end of history" or "the clash of civilizations". These stories need exotic seasonings, and the native informers provide them. They are the byproduct of an international intellectual free trade, in which intellectual carpetbaggers offer their services to the highest bidder, for the lowest risk.

In making this argument, I do not intend to personalize the native informers. The names I have mentioned—Azar Nafisi, Ibn

Warraq, and so on—are sites not citations, personas not persons. I hold their writings and other utterances responsible for having helped dehumanize populations that can then be murdered—by the hundreds in Palestine, the thousands in Lebanon, the hundreds of thousands in Iraq—with total impunity. I feel pain in giving them names, for in the figure of the native informer the fictive white man presiding in their mind and soul has stolen me from me. He has owned up to robbing me from me and can now talk back to me in my own language, the language I thought I had successfully hidden from him so that I could speak freedom. I now speak, but I sound exactly like the native informer, for he sits there in and with a position of power—over me. By becoming a house Muslim he has cast me into the site of the field Muslim. I look at the native informer, at the Muslim native informer, and once again I am ashamed of me—for in him I see me subjected, defeated, humiliated, embarrassed. I fight a fight he has already conceded, she has already lost—lost so completely she does not even remember the fight. It took me a long time not to be ashamed of me—it took from Gandhi to Mandela, from Martin Luther King to Malcolm X, from Che Guevara to Frantz Fanon, from Aimé Césaire to Edward Said; and now, once again, the fictive white man uses me, abuses me, uses his native informer, Cain to my Abel—who looks and speaks exactly like me—to make me ashamed of me. I take in the native informer, his image, her picture, his writing, her accent—and I see me, degraded, degenerated, turned against me, exactly at the moment when I rise to denounce him, to shame her. He is the I I had in me when I was silent; I am the me she had in her when she was unknown. I look at him now, and all I see is a replica of me, my carbon copy, talking back at and against me—not just my split but also my splitting persona—overinterpreting me as a character and a culture, by way of killing my fighting instincts.

Sometimes a cigar is just a cigar, as the supreme symbolist of our psyche once said, and sometimes a pair of innocent-looking shoes is all you have to throw at the cruel fate facing you. Do not interpret the world, a man in German shoes once said—change it! In the final analysis neither should the native informer be demonized nor the recodification of racism fetishized. False consciousness is just how commodity fetishization and alienation operate. But in my mirror, the native informer cannot hide, for in his mirror I have shown him his face—taken the white mask off his brown skin.

HOME IS HERE, NEVER IS NOW: CONFUSING THE COLOR LINE

The recodification of racism in North America (and, by extension, Western Europe) is an exceedingly important and historic development, for from our vantage point it in fact, and quite paradoxically, defetishizes the famous color line that W. E. B. Du Bois identified as the defining moment of the twentieth century; and it exposes the social construction of racism and the manufactured racialization of humanity, thus divided so that it may be better ruled. With the services they are eager to provide, the native informers present a paradoxically positive aspect, for they become caricatures of themselves by caricaturing the cultures they represent or misrepresent. By overselling themselves, the native informers expose the transitory paradigmatics of manufacturing race, ethnicity, and gender apartheid mechanisms. The color line can no longer claim to be the defining moment of the twentieth century with Barack Obama as president and, more important, with the transmutation of black into brown, African into Arab, and Jew into Muslim. This transitional period exposes the naked neurosis of the racist imagination and should release humanity forever from the artificial bondage of manufactured racialization, of racialized minorities (who are in fact the majority), cross-fetishizing their "races". For every black or brown native informer there are millions of human beings who are not and should not be trapped inside a racialized imagination. The transitory transmutation of black into brown and Jew into Muslim more than anything else exposes the transparency of the fictive white man who stands at the center of this racialized imagination.

The central challenge to this emancipation from a murderous racialized delusion is the position of power in which the fictive white man has posited himself as the defining center and cast humanity at large as his periphery. No more treacherous traps reinforce this false, falsifying, and disabling binary than the persistently alienating notions of exile and diaspora. Rich Iranians in Los Angeles or London, Palestinians in Chile or Paris, or Cubans in Florida are neither in exile nor of the diaspora; they are perfectly at home right where they are. Exile and diaspora must be retained for Palestinians in derelict refugee camps in Lebanon, where they share their misery with millions of illegal migrant laborers from the four corners of the world. The rapid rise in legal and illegal migrant workers around the globe (there are almost 300 million of them, according to UN—

equal to the population of the United States) has cast the notion of "home" severely off balance.[33]

So where is home now, and who is at home, and why does it matter? In what she calls "the virtualized demographic frontiers of the modern world", Gayatri Spivak has opted to be "in both worlds"—India and America—"deeply, without being quite of them. I believe that slight anomaly gives us a certain distance, which may be valuable".[34] But being in two worlds one is in neither, and the "slight anomaly" is no longer sufficient for the critical affinity we need with where and what we are. If any measure of "anomaly" is to constitute critical distance, then it must be internal to the voice that dissents, not to the accent that alienates. Spivak identifies herself among the "theoreticians of migrant hybridity".[35] Not any longer. Not when—immigrant or citizen—your tax money builds bombs and drops them on your brothers and sisters halfway around the globe, in Afghanistan, Iraq, Lebanon, and Palestine. "Theoretical hybridity" dissolves in the face of the income-tax reports one must file every April 15. The only people entitled to "theoretical hybridity" are illegal immigrants, who do not pay taxes. In the face of determined barbarities made possible by my tax money, I can no longer be a "theoretician of migrant hybridity", or, even worse, a hybridity, a migrant, myself. I am here, and here is home— unfetishized, deromanticized, cut loose from all nostalgia—and I am here to stay, for my children are here, and here I have a fight to fight. One way I have found to kill the market for the native informers is to feel and be at home right here where I am, where we are, where they are, and to think and act in a manner, as if I belonged—and that "as if" is enough for me. I am on loan here. If, in addition to my American passport, I have earned the wrath of racist Americans—of the neoconservatives who take my brown for their black, my Muslim for their Jew—more than I have achieved the support of their liberal counterparts, then that in and of itself is a beginning. I am of this land not by virtue of a father who came here before me, but by virtue of the four children who were born here after I arrived, whom I have fathered while a sojourner in this unacknowledged gift of native Americans. To put the native informer out of business, I must become native to that America and inform it otherwise, force the native informers to take off their white masks and teach them how to see their brown skin, their fair share in the colorful cascade of humanity.

"In the era of breakneck globalization," Spivak says, "I propose the planet to overwrite the globe ... The planet is in the species of alterity, belonging to another system; and yet we inhabit it, on loan."[36] Yes, fine—on loan. But alterity is not ulterior. Alterity is interior. The logic of the dialectic demands that it be. "In order to think the migrant as well as the recipient of foreign aid, we must think the other. To think the other, as everyone knows, is one meaning of being human. To be human is to be intended toward the other ... It is only then that we will be able to think the migrant as well as the recipient of foreign aid in the species of alterity, not simply as the white person's burden."[37] This is a bit too Christian, especially coming from a Hindu, as she distances herself from Kipling. Instead, let us rethink the immigrant—for in the United States everyone is an immigrant, though some have repressed that truth (and others are constantly reminded of it): some came here by boat, others by jumbo jet; some crossed the border, while for others the border crossed them.

We are no longer in diaspora. We must all be at home where we are. I live in New York City, whose leading newspaper, the *New York Times*, has a columnist named Thomas Friedman, who wrote a column, two weeks into the massacre of Palestinians in Gaza, in which he held that the slaughter of Palestinians would teach them a lesson. Drawing a comparison with the Israeli massacre of Lebanese civilians in 2006, Friedman wrote, "Israel basically said that when dealing with a nonstate actor, Hezbollah, nested among civilians, the only long-term source of deterrence was to exact enough pain on the civilians—the families and employers of the militants—to restrain Hezbollah in the future." Driving his point home, he then adds, "In Gaza, I still can't tell if Israel is trying to eradicate Hamas or trying to 'educate' Hamas, by inflicting a heavy death toll on Hamas militants and heavy pain on the Gaza population. If it is out to destroy Hamas, casualties will be horrific and the aftermath could be Somalia-like chaos. If it is out to educate Hamas, Israel may have achieved its aims." Is this not incitement to murder, verbal glee at the sight of slaughter, reminiscent of the young Israelis who picnic while watching their army massacre Palestinians?[38] Inflicting death and destruction as a way of "educating" the Palestinians—is this not "Arbeit macht frei" in American English? If a Muslim were to make the same claim about Israelis that Friedman makes about Palestinians—that inflicting pain and suffering, death and destruction, is teaching them a lesson, is "educating" them—he would be on his way to Guantanamo Bay by now. This is the difference between being a Jew and a Muslim in New York—when the Muslim of 2000s America has become the Jew of 1930s Germany.[39]

In this city, with that newspaper and that columnist, I must and I do feel at home, for if I feel soiled after reading Thomas Friedman's work I can go and take a cleansing shower in the poetry of Yehuda Amichai, whom I also discovered here in New York, in English. I am not an alien here—not anymore. I am not alienated. I am not in exile. I am not in diaspora. I am home here, more than anything else by virtue of the fact that Thomas Friedman and the native informers he loves to quote enable me to fight back—and I owe that fight to my children, my four American children, whom the Israelis and their Zionist supporters in the United States cannot murder with impunity. I am not an American by birth. My children are American—and I am here to fight for an America in which they can pronounce their beautiful Persian names—Kaveh, Pardis, Chelgis, and Golchin—with pride, while the suffering of countless children in Afghanistan, in Iraq, in Lebanon, and in Palestine weighs heavy on their parents' hearts.

I live in a city where, if after the Israelis massacre Palestinians by the hundreds and maim them for life by the thousands, a handful of souls dare to demonstrate in protest, the police attack them with mace tear gas sprays, charge at them on horseback, arrest and jail them.[40] And yet in this same city, thousands of pro-Israeli demonstrators gather to cheer the Israeli army to kill more Palestinians, with the governor of the state and one of its senators joining in.[41] In the city where I live I have seen my picture cut out to make me look like a two-headed monster, splashed on the cover of local tabloids where journalists have attacked and criminalized me merely because I dared to put together a Palestinian film festival. In this city I feel at home, I have a cause, my life has a purpose—I have a band of native informers to expose. I live in a country where I dare not send a few hundred dollars to a charitable organization in Gaza to help care for people slaughtered by Israel for fear of being accused of aiding and abetting terrorism; yet in this very country billions of dollars of the tax money collected from citizens like me are sent on a regular basis to the supreme terrorist organization on the planet, which goes by the name "Israel", to maim and murder my brothers and sisters in Palestine. In this city and in this country I must and I defiantly do feel at home. I feel at home here because this is where Malcolm X was born and raised and gunned down. In his homeland I feel at home. In his defiance he has enabled me to rise and stand up to barbarity and stake my own claim on Langston

Hughes, and add the name of my Karun River to his chorus when he sings, in "The Negro Speaks of Rivers" (1922),

> I bathed in the Euphrates when dawns were young.
> I built my hut near the Congo and it lulled me to sleep.
> I looked upon the Nile and raised the pyramids above it.
> I heard the singing of the Mississippi when Abe Lincoln went
>   down ...

From the Karun to the Mississippi to the Hudson: I am here to stay, for I live in a city to which I have added my color to the colorful curiosities of its pavements. We colorful folks came to this country—we Arabs, Iranians, Turks, Afghans, Pakistanis, Indians, Latinos and Latinas—and we confused its color lines. We laughed when people called each other white or black, for we were neither, for we were both, for we began to get under their skins—white and black. The black people thought we were white; the white people thought we were black. We were neither. We were both. We are chameleons. We had brought color and race into ocular revolt. We confused their demarcations. We are chameleons—the nightmares of aging racists who did not know quite what to do with us and dismissed us as "sand niggers"—and we laughed, oh how happy it made us to be made of sand, sadness, sorrow, songs of courage and guts, lyrics of revolt.

We forever confused the color line and exposed the sheer stupidity of that dark dividing line that made some people white and others black. Black? They were light or dark chocolatey brown. White? They were yellowish or pinkish, not white. White? Kaqaz-e espid e na-benveshteh bash—we began teaching the Persian that Rumi wrote and spoke: "O brother be an unwritten blank page of paper." As on paper, so on human beings can just about anything be written. We the unwritten, we began to write ourselves, in jest, in gestures, in frivolity, with gesticulations that mocked the seriousness of the color line. "The problem of the twentieth century," wrote W. E. B. Dubois, "is the problem of the color line—the relation of the darker to the lighter races of men in Asia and Africa, in America and the islands of the seas." Not anymore, not in the twenty-first century. We have made sure of it. We colorful folks confuse the color line, so that white and black folks no longer know which is which, for we are neither, we are both. We are full and free of color. We are free. We the unwritten blank pages of ourselves, waiting to be written and read by the posterity we have bred in this world—our children, and our children's children; we will grow, and we will prosper, and we will become more. Those nameless children the Israelis just massacred in Gaza—we have bred them back here in America. We joggle, we dodge, we hide, we come back. Millions and millions more Palestinian children have poured dancing into the sea from the shores of Gaza, and they are sailing—see the masts of their boats! They are coming. They are coming home. Welcome to America! Welcome home!

Glossary

Alienation – the state or experience of being isolated from a group or an activity to which one should belong or in which one should be involved, or a feeling of estrangement. In psychiatry, it is a state of depersonalization or loss of identity in which the self seems unreal, thought to be caused by difficulties in relating to society and the resulting prolonged inhibition of emotion. The root of Fanon's conceptualization was medical, he meant a neurosis.

Al Qaeda – (meaning "the base") this is a militant Islamic group founded between August 1988 and late 1989. It purportedly operates as a network comprising both a multinational, stateless army and a fundamentalist Sunni movement calling for global Jihad. Al-Qaeda ideologues envision a complete break from foreign influences in Muslim countries and the creation of a new Islamic caliphate. Al-Qaeda has attacked civilian and military targets in various countries.

Alterity – the state of being "other" or different. It means "otherness" and originates from late Latin alteritas, from alter "other".

Analogon – Jean Paul Sartre said that what is required for the imaginary process to occur is an analogon—that is, an equivalent of perception. This can be a painting, a photograph, a sketch, or even the mental image we conjure when we think of someone or something. Through the imaginary process, the analogon loses its own sense and takes on the sense of the object it represents. An analogon can take on new qualities based on one's own intention toward it.

Anomie – a lack of the usual social or ethical standards in an individual or group. Durkheim defined the term anomie as a condition where social and/or moral norms are confused, unclear, or simply not present. Durkheim felt that this lack of norms—or pre-accepted limits on behavior in society—led to deviant behavior. Industrialization in particular, according to Durkheim, tends to dissolve restraints on the passions of humans. Where traditional societies, primarily through religion, successfully taught people to control their desires and goals, he felt that modern industrial societies separated people and weakened social bonds as a result of increased complexity and the division of labor.

Arbeit macht frei – is a German phrase that can be translated as "work will make you free", "work liberates" or "work makes one free". The expression comes from the title of an 1873 novel by German philologist Lorenz Diefenbach, in which gamblers and fraudsters find the path to virtue through labour. The phrase was adopted in 1928 by the Weimar government as a slogan extolling the effects of their large-scale public works programmes to end unemployment. It was continued in this usage by the Nazi Party when it came to power in 1933 and it was later placed at the entrances to a number of Nazi Concentration Camps.

Ayn – (Ayin) is a letter that appears in many Semitic languages, including Phoenician, Aramaic, Hebrew, and Arabic. It is also the twenty-first letter in the new Persian alphabet. It represents a sound which has no equivalent in English. The Maltese language, which uses a Latin alphabet, writes the ayin as għ.

Bête noire – a person or thing that one particularly dislikes. Its origins lie in the mid nineteenth century and the French term for "black beast".

Carpetbagger – This word can mean a political candidate who seeks election in an area where they have no local connections. Or, for example, when used historically (in the US), it can mean a person from the northern states who went to the South after the Civil War to profit from the reconstruction. It can also mean a person perceived as an unscrupulous opportunist.

Chutzpah – shameless audacity; impudence. The word originates from Yiddish.

Civilizational thinking – while European national cultures were concocted to distinguish one economic unit of capital from another, civilizational thinking was invented to unify these cultures against their colonial consequences. Islamic, Indian, or African civilizations were invented contrapuntally by Orientalism…in order to match, balance and thus authenticate "Western Civilization".

CliffsNotes – literature notes and study guides that US students from junior high to graduate school have been turning to in order to save study time since 1958. They are advertised as "written by real teachers and professors".

Coloniality – the "coloniality of power" is an expression coined by Anibal Quijano to name the structures of power, control, and hegemony that have emerged during the modernist era, the era of colonialism, which stretches from the conquest of the Americas to the present.

Comprador (also compradore) – this Portuguese word dates from 1840 and refers to a Chinese agent engaged by a European business interest in China to oversee its native employees and to act as an intermediary in its business affairs. Later, it was extended to refer to any native servant in the service of a colonial commercial interest who would purchase necessaries and keep the household accounts: a house-steward.

Connoted – the implied or suggested (idea or feeling) in addition to the literal or primary meaning of a word. It can also imply as a consequence or condition associated with a fact. Connote refers to other characteristics suggested or implied by that thing, not the inherent characteristics of that thing.

Cosmogonic – an adjective derived from the branch of science that deals with the origin of the universe, especially the solar system.

Disalienation – Frantz Fanon advocated the stripping away of the social conditions that cause alienation. He calls for the stripping away of the "white mask", or false consciousness, thereby bringing about a reintegration of the real self. He called this process disalienation.

Fat'ha – In the Arabic language, fat'ha indicates a short vowel sound, that is pronounced right after the letter it is on. It looks like a line over a letter and makes the short "a" sound. The line is sometimes horizontal, but it is usually slanted. It is never vertical. It is a diacritic. Fat'ha is not always written. Its main use is in words the reader is not familiar with, in order to ensure the reader pronounces it correctly.

Hamas – takes its name from the Arabic initials for the Islamic Resistance Movement. Designated a terrorist organization by Israel, the US and the EU, Hamas is seen by its supporters as a legitimate fighting force defending Palestinians from a brutal military occupation. It was formed in 1987 at the beginning of the first intifada, or Palestinian uprising, against Israel's occupation in the West Bank and Gaza.

Hamza – (al-hamza) is a letter in the Arabic alphabet, representing the glottal stop. Hamza is not one of the 28 "full" letters, and owes its existence to historical orthographical inconsistencies in early Islamic times. The hamza can be written alone or with a carrier, in which case it becomes a diacritic.

Hegemony – the predominant influence, as of a state, region, or group, over another or others. It can refer to political, economic, ideological or cultural power exerted by a dominant group over other groups, regardless of the explicit consent of the latter.

Hermeneutics – the branch of knowledge that deals with interpretation, especially of the Bible or literary texts.

Hezbollah – a Shi'a Islamist political and paramilitary organization in Lebanon.

Hochkultur – a German word meaning very advanced civilization or very high culture.

Homo sacer – According to Italian philosopher Giorgio Agamben, homo sacer is an individual who exists in the law as an exile. But, the paradox is that it is only because of the law that society can recognize the individual as homo sacer, and so the law that mandates the exclusion is also what gives the individual an identity. Agamben holds that life exists in two capacities. One is natural biological life (Greek: Zoë) and the other is political life (Greek: bios). The effect of homo sacer is, he says, a schism of one's biological and political lives. So, as "bare life", the homo sacer finds that, although he has biological life, it has no political significance. Further in his work, Agamben describes the status of those prisoners at Guantanamo Bay, Cuba under confinement by the United States as being contemporary examples similar to the Jews during the Holocaust.

Idiot savant – a person who is considered to be mentally handicapped but displays brilliance in a specific area, especially one involving memory. It is from the French, literally meaning "learned idiot".

Imperium – an age when there was a feeling of empowerment: absolute power. It originates from the Latin for "command", "authority" and "empire".

Infomercial – a television programme that promotes a product in an informative and supposedly objective way.

Irtidad – This is Arabic for apostasizing. The Arabic word for an apostasy is *ridda*. A person is an apostate if they leave a religion and either adopt another religion or assume a patently non-religious lifestyle. Historically, Islam, Christianity and other religions have taken a very dim view of apostates. They were often executed. Apostasy in Islam is currently a very complex and sensitive issue. Some schools of Islamic jurisprudence still say that apostasy by a male Muslim is punishable by death, although that penalty is very rarely carried out nowadays. Opinions differ as to whether women should be executed or given time in jail to repent. But viewpoints on apostasy differ widely across the Muslim world. Some Muslims believe that apostasy laws are not derived from the Quran. Other Muslims simply do not support the apostasy penalty; many of them openly condemn it. Some scholars say a Muslim is free to convert out of Islam if they choose to, but if a Muslim converts then speaks against Islam then that is considered as treason. Beliefs and attitudes vary.

Islamophobia – a hatred or fear of Islam or Muslims, especially when feared as a political force.

Jihadism – In Arabic, the word jihad is a noun meaning "struggle". Jihad appears frequently in the Quran and common usage as the idiomatic expression "striving in the way of Allah". A wide range of opinions exist about the exact meaning of jihad. Muslims use the word in a religious context to refer to three types of struggles: an internal struggle to maintain faith, the struggle to improve the Muslim society, or the struggle in a holy war. The differences of opinion are the result of different interpretation of the two most important sources in Islam, the

Quran and the ahadith (singular: hadith). But, in Western societies the term jihad is often automatically translated as "holy war". Muslim authors tend to reject such an approach, stressing non-militant connotations of the word.

Kaffeeklatsch – an informal social gathering at which coffee is served. Talking or gossip is usually much in evidence at such gatherings. The word's origins lie in the German *Kaffee*, meaning "coffee", and *Klatsch*, meaning "gossip".

Kiarostami – Abbas Kiarostami, who was born in 1940, is an internationally acclaimed Iranian film-maker, director, screenwriter, photographer and film-producer. An active film-maker since 1970, Kiarostami has been involved in more than 40 films. He is also a poet, photographer, painter, illustrator, and graphic designer. He is part of a generation of film-makers in the Iranian New Wave, a Persian cinema movement that started in the late 1960s. The film-makers share many common techniques including the use of poetic dialogue and allegorical storytelling dealing with political and philosophical issues.

Lactification – this is the word Frantz Fanon used to describe the desire to "whiten the race". By analyzing these types of phenomena, Fanon meant to liberate "the man of color from himself", to achieve "the effective disalienation of the black man".

Leitmotif – a recurrent theme throughout a musical or literary composition, associated with a particular person, idea, or situation. The word originates from the nineteenth century German word *Leitmotiv*.

Martinican – (Martiniquan) person who hails from Martinique, an island in the eastern Caribbean sea, with a land area of 436 square miles. It is an overseas region of France. To the north-west lies Dominica, to the south St Lucia, and to the south-east Barbados. As with the other overseas departments, Martinique is one of the 26 regions of France and an integral part of the Republic. As part of France, Martinique is part of the European Union, and its currency is the Euro. Its official language is French, although many of its inhabitants also speak Antillean Creole.

Madrasa – usually a college for Islamic instruction. In Arabic, the word simply means "school".

Métropole – from the Greek 'metropolis', meaning mother city (polis being a city state, hence the word is also used for any colonizing 'mother country'). For example, London became the metropole of the British Empire, insofar as its politicians and businessmen determined the economic, diplomatic, and military character of the rest of the Empire. By contrast, the periphery was the rest of the Empire, outside the British Isles themselves. The traditional view is that the British Empire was constituted by the formal control of territories, by direct governance of foreign lands, instigated by the metropole.

Mi'raj – a part of the journey Muhammad took in one night on a winged horse around the year 621. Most Muslims consider it a physical journey, while others say it happened spiritually through a metaphorical vision. Some scholars consider the *Mi'raj* a dream or vision. Other Muslims say that when Muhammad ascended it was a physical journey until he reached the farthest lote tree, a tree in the Seventh Heaven beyond which no angel is allowed to cross, on the other side of which is the throne of God.

Mission civilisatrice – is French and refers to the white civilizing mission. As the primary rationalization for colonialism, the "civilizing mission" signified France's attempt to convert its colonial subjects into French people. Whereas the British tended to reject the notion that an Indian, for example, might become British, the French believed that if properly taught French values and the French language,

Algerians and Vietnamese alike would slowly evolve and become French. Hence the term evolué, which was used to refer to those who had adapted to French culture. There was also a moral component to the civilizing mission, in that some French held that it was their duty as a more enlightened race to elevate the ignorant masses of the non-Western world.

Mosharekat – this was the name of the leading reformist newspaper in Iran. This newspaper was published by a political party, the Islamic Iran Participation Front, but was banned along with 13 other reformist newspapers in April, 2000. While still backing Islam, the state religion of Iran, The Islamic Iran Participation Front is actually among the pioneers of democracy in Iran.

Mukhtar – village or town headman or chief.

Mullah – a Muslim learned in Islamic theology and sacred law. The words origins lie in the early seventeenth century. It comes from the Persian, Turkish, and Urdu word "mullā", and from the Arabic "mawlā", meaning "vicar", "master" and "guardian". In large parts of the Muslim world, particularly Iran, Bosnia, Afghanistan, Turkey, Central Asia and the Indian subcontinent, it is the name commonly given to local Islamic clerics or mosque leaders.

Nemesis – (the plural is Nemeses) nowadays, the term commonly refers to an arch-enemy. But the word originally meant the distributor of fortune, neither good nor bad, simply in due proportion to each according to his deserts. Later, nemesis came to suggest the resentment caused by any disturbance of this right proportion, the sense of justice which could not allow it to pass unpunished. The word originates from the Greek goddess named Nemesis, who was the spirit of divine retribution against those who succumb to hubris (arrogance before the gods). The name Nemesis is related to the Greek word *némein*, meaning "to give what is due".

Negritude – the quality or fact of being of black African origin, or the affirmation or consciousness of the value of black or African culture, heritage, and identity. The word originates from *négritude*, the French word for "blackness".

Neoliberalism – refers to a set of economic policies that have become widespread during the last 25 years. In theory, it is about making trade between nations easier—about the free movement of goods, resources and enterprises in a bid to always find cheaper resources, to maximize profits and efficiency. To help accomplish this, neoliberalism requires the removal of various controls deemed as barriers to free trade. The goal is to be able to to allow the free market to naturally balance itself via the pressures of market demands. But, in reality, under neoliberalism, the rich tend to grow richer and the poor grow poorer.

Neoconservatism – neoconservatives generally advocate a free-market economy with minimum taxation and government economic regulation, strict limits on government-provided social-welfare programs, and a strong military supported by large defense budgets. They tend to maintain that the US should take an active role in world affairs, though they are generally suspicious of international institutions, such as the United Nations, whose authority could intrude upon American sovereignty or limit the country's freedom to act in its own interests.

Nakba – (*El Nakba*) Arabic for "the catastrophe" or what the Palestinians call the events of 1948, whereby they were driven from their villages in acts of ethnic cleansing.

Orientalism – the knowledge and study of the languages and cultures of the peoples of west, east or central Asia. It can also mean something considered characteristic of such people.

Op-Ed – a type of article that includes commentary and is usually printed on the page opposite the editorial page in a newspaper.

Phantasm – a figment of the imagination, an illusion or apparition. It can also mean an illusory likeness of something.

Phantasmagoric – a sequence of real or imaginary images like that seen in a dream.

Plangent – an adjective usually denoting the loud, reverberating, and often melancholy qualities of a sound.

Ponzi scheme – a fraudulent investment operation that pays returns to separate investors from their own money or money paid by subsequent investors, rather than from any actual profit earned. It usually offers abnormally high or unusually consistent short-term returns. The perpetuation of the payouts requires an ever-increasing flow of money from investors and the scheme will eventually collapse under its own weight. The 2009 case of Bernard Madoff demonstrates the ability of such a scheme to delude both individual and institutional investors as well as securities authorities for long periods. The scheme is named after Charles Ponzi, who became notorious for using the technique in early 1920. But Ponzi did not invent it. For example, Charles Dickens' 1857 novel Little Dorrit described such a scheme.

Postmodernism – a late twentieth century strand of thought that represents a departure from modernism and has at its heart a general distrust of grand theories and ideologies. It is a tendency in contemporary culture characterised by the rejection of objective truth and global cultural narrative. It emphasises the role of language, power relations, and motivations; in particular it attacks the use of sharp classifications such as male versus female, straight versus gay, white versus black, and imperial versus colonial. It has influenced many cultural fields, including literary criticism, sociology, linguistics, architecture, visual arts, and music.

Referent – In linguistics, means the thing that a word or phrase denotes or stands for. For example, "the Morning Star" and "the Evening Star" have the same referent, the planet Venus.

Ridda – this is the Arabic noun for apostasy. (See also *Irtidad* above.)

Shoa – (Sho'ah and Shoah) the biblical word Shoa, meaning "catastrophe, calamity, disaster, and destruction", became the standard Hebrew term for the Holocaust as early as the 1940s. Holocaust was also sometimes adopted as a translation of Shoa.

Simulacrum – comes from the Latin word simulacrum, which means "likeness" or "similarity". The word is first recorded in the English language in the late sixteenth century, and is used to describe a representation of another thing, such as a statue or a painting—especially of a god. By the late nineteenth century, it had gathered a secondary association of inferiority: an image without the substance or qualities of the original.

Taliban – (Taleban) this is a Sunni Islamist political movement that governed Afghanistan from 1996 until it was overthrown in late 2001. It has regrouped since 2004 and revived as a strong insurgency movement governing mainly local Pashtun areas and fighting a guerilla war against the governments of Afghanistan, Pakistan, and the NATO-led International Security Assistance Force (ISAF). It is primarily made up of members belonging to ethnic Pashtun tribes along with volunteers from nearby Islamic countries. Its main leader is Mullah Muhammed Omar.

Ten-percenter – this denotes a person who takes commission at a specified rate.

Wahabi – *Wahhabism* is a conservative Sunni Islamic sect based on the teachings of Muhammad Ibn Abd-al-Wahhab, an eighteenth century scholar from what is today known as Saudi Arabia, who wanted to purge Islam of what he considered innovations in Islam. *Wahhabism* is the dominant form of Islam in Saudi Arabia. The primary doctrine of *Wahhabi* is Tawhid or the uniqueness and unity of God. The term *Wahhabi* was first used by opponents of Muhammad Ibn-al-Wahhab. It is considered derogatory by the people it is used to describe, who prefer to be called "unitarians" (*Muwahiddun*).

Weltliteratur – Johann Wolfgang von Goethe introduced the concept of *Weltliteratur* in 1827 to describe the growing availability of texts from other nations, including translations from Sanskrit, Islamic and Serbian epic poetry. Karl Marx and Friedrich Engels used the term in their Communist Manifesto (1848) to describe the "cosmopolitan character" of bourgeois literary production.

Notes

INTRODUCTION: INFORMING EMPIRES

1. For further informed speculations about those responsible for the carnage, pointing the finger at the internal politics of India, See Tariq Ali's "The Assault on Mumbai", *Counterpunch*, November 27, 2008, available at www. counterpunch.org/trichromatic—accessed on December 3, 2008.
2. The most detailed account of the incidents in Mumbai was reported by the BBC at http://news.bbc.co.uk/1/hi/world/south_asia/7756321.stm—accessed November 29, 2009.
3. For a critical take on the Mumbai attack, particularly an insightful comparison of the life of tourists with that of the ordinary and impoverished Indians, see Arundhati Roy, "The monster in the mirror", *Guardian*, December 13, 2008, available at www.guardian.co.uk/world/2008/dec/12/mumbai-arundhati-roy—accessed on January 13, 2009.
4. See Sarah Boseley's article on the *Lancet* report, "655,000 Iraqis killed since invasion", *Guardian*, October 11, 2006, available at: www.guardian.co.uk/world/2006/oct/11/iraq.iraq—accessed November 29, 2008. "Although such death rates might be common in times of war," the authors of the *Lancet* report, Gilbert Burnham and colleagues, were reported to have said, "The combination of a long duration and tens of millions of people affected has made this the deadliest international conflict of the 21st century and should be of grave concern to everyone."
5. For a report on the Hadithah massacre, which has been compared to the Mai Lai massacre in Vietnam in 1969, also committed by the US Marines, see Suzanne Goldenberg, "Marines may face trial over Iraq massacre", *Guardian*, May 27, 2006, available at www.guardian.co.uk/world/2006/may/27/iraq.topstories3—accessed on November 29, 2009.
6. Thomas L. Friedman, "Calling all Pakistanis", *New York Times*, December 2, 2008), available at www.nytimes.com/2008/12/03/opinion/03friedman.html—accessed on December 3, 2008.
7. Friedman, "Calling all Pakistanis".
8. See Amira Haas, "Don't shoot till you can see they're over the age of 12", *Ha'aretz*, November 20, 2000.
9. For a detailed analysis of Judith Miller's reports from Iraq when embedded with the US forces, and how those reports mislead the American public into believing Saddam Hussein had amassed weapons of mass destructions see Herbert L. Abrams, "WMD: Weapons of Miller's Descriptions", *Bulletin of Atomic Scientists*, Vol. 60, No. 4, July/August 2004: 56–64.
10. For a detailed discussion of the lack of neutrality of the *New York Times* over the Afghan and Iraq wars, see Howard Friel and Richard Falk, *The Record of the Paper: How the New York Times Misreports US Foreign Policy* (London and New York: Verso, 2007).

11. For more details on why and how Alan Dershowitz thinks torture ought to be legalized, see his *Why Terrorism Works* (New Haven, CT: Yale University Press, 2002).

12. For more details see Michael Ignatieff, *The Lesser Evil: Political Ethics in an Age of Terror* (Princeton: Princeton University Press, 2004).

13. For more details on "Obsession" and its neoconservative and Israeli links, see Adam Shatz, "Short Cuts", *London Review of Books*, October 9, 2008.

14. See William Kornhauser, *The Politics of Mass Society* (New York: The Free Press, 1959).

15. See Guy Debord, *The Society of the Spectacle*. Translated by Ken Knabb. (Oakland, CA: AKPress, 2006).

16. For more on Robert Bellah's concept of "civil religion" see his "Civil religion in America", *Journal of the American Academy of Arts and Sciences* (96: 1, Winter 1967): 1–21. See also Robert N. Bellah, *Beyond Belief: Essays on Religion in a Post-Traditionalist World* (Berkeley, CA: University of California Press, 1991).

17. Alexis de Tocqueville, *Democracy in America*, translated by George Lawrence and edited by J. P. Mayer (New York: Anchor Books, 1969): 254–5.

18. Tocqueville, *Democracy in America*: 255–6.

19. I have made a preliminary sketch of reading John Ford's cinema as a template of American empire in my essay, "The American Empire: Triumph of Triumphalism", *Unbound: Harvard Journal of the Legal Left*, Vol. 4, No. 82, 2008.

20. See Walter Nugent, *Habits of Empire: A History of American Expansion* (New York: Alfred A. Knopf, 2008). Chalmers Johnson's *Blowback Trilogy* began with his *Blowback: The Costs and Consequences of American Empire* (New York: Henry Holt, 2000), and after the events of 9/11 continued first with *The Sorrows of Empire: Militarism, Secrecy, and the End of the Republic* (New York: Henry Holt, 2004) and finally with *Nemesis: The Last Days of the American Republic* (New York: Henry Holt, 2006). I have covered the most recent surge of literature on American imperialism in my essay "The American Empire: Triumph of Triumphalism".

21. See my "For the Last Time: Civilizations", *International Sociology*, September 2001. Vol. 16, No. 3: 361–8.

22. These statistics are the subject of much lamentation by Peter Brimelow, himself a British émigré to the US, in his *Alien Nation: Common Sense About America's Immigration Disaster* (New York: Harper, 1996).

23. The campus of my own university, Columbia, has been a major battlefield. For two representative examples of the lucrative, anti-intellectual, McCarthyite genre attacking what in the US passes for "the left" in the academy, see Roger Kimball, *Tenured Radicals: How Politics Has Corrupted Our Higher Education* (Chicago, IL: Ivan R. Dee, 2008), and David Horowitz, *The Professors: The 101 Most Dangerous Academics in America* (Washington, DC: Regnery, 2007).

24. For more on Leo Strauss and his link to American neo-conservatism, see Anne Norton, *Leo Strauss and the Politics of American Empire* (New Haven: Yale University Press, 2005). For a shorter but equally compelling account, see Earl Shorris, "Ignoble Liars: Leo Strauss, George Bush, and the Philosophy of Mass Deception" (*Harper's*, January 2004).

25. For a detailed examination of the link between Leo Strauss and Karl Schmitt, see Heinrich Meier, *Carl Schmidt and Leo Strauss: The Hidden Dialogue* (Chicago: University of Chicago Press, 1988/1995).

26. For the central significance of the constitution of "the enemy" in Karl Schmitt's political theory, see his *Concept of the Political* (Chicago: University of Chicago Press, 2007).

27. There has been a widespread criticism of Azar Nafisi's *Reading Lolita in Tehran* by Iranian women in and out of their homeland. For a representative sample by Iranian women scholars, see Negar Mottahedeh, "Off the grid: Reading Iranian memoirs in our time of total war" (MERIP, 2004); Roksana Bahramitash, "The War on Terror, Feminist Orientalism, and Orientalist Feminism", *Critique: Critical Middle Eastern Studies*, 14, 2005: 221–35; Mitra Rastegar, "Reading Nafisi in the West: Authenticity, Orientalism, and 'Liberating' Iranian Women", *Women's Studies Quarterly* 34: 1 and 2, Spring/ Summer 2006: 108–28); Fatemeh Keshavarz, *Jasmine and Stars: Reading More Than Lolita in Tehran* (Chapel Hill, NC: The University of North Carolina Press, 2007); and Farzaneh Milani, "On Women's Captivity in the Islamic World", *MERIP* 246, Spring 2008. Leili Golafshani's 2008 doctoral dissertation at the University of Queensland in Brisbane, Australia, is the most recent critical assessment of Nafisi's memoir.

28. See Adam Shatz's "The Native Informant", *The Nation*, April 10, 2003.

29. See Gayatri Chakravorty Spivak, *A Critique of Postcolonial Reason: Toward a History of the Vanishing Present* (Cambridge, MA: Harvard University Press, 1999): ix.

30. See Mahmut Mutman, "Writing Culture: Postmodernism and Ethnography", *Anthropological Theory* Volume 6, No. 2, 2006: 153–78.

31. See George Marcus, "How Anthropological Curiosity Consumes Its Own Places of Origin", *Cultural Anthropology* 1999: Vol. 14, No. 3: 416–22; and Nicholas de Genova, "The State of an Anthropology of the United States", *CR: The New Centennial Review*, Vol. 7, No. 2, 2007, pp. 231–77.

32. For two representative examples of this sort of anthropology, see Nadje Al-Ali's *Iraqi Women: Untold Stories From 1948 to the Present* (London: Zed, 2007), and Pardis Mahdavi's *Passionate Uprisings: Iran's Sexual Revolution* (Stanford: Stanford University Press, 2008). In the first instance, the native informant turned anthropologist partakes in the deep colonial grammar of her discipline (always an anthropology of the Other) and turns the members of her own immediate family, friends, and acquaintances into objects of anthropological curiosity and sophomoric theorization, and in the second into sexual objects of a similarly dehumanizing gaze. What these and similar anthropologists are doing, conducting their "field work" without even noting the military origin of what they do, amounts to "biopiracy" of the profoundest sort: stealing people's stories to conjugate the deep grammar of anthropological colonialism beyond the white man's reach. For an alternative take on the predicament of Iraqi woman, by a courageous and eloquent Iraqi woman activist, see the extraordinary text of Haifa Zangana, *An Iraqi Woman's Account of War and Resistance* (New York: Seven Stories, 2007).

33. For more details of the function of this PR firm, see Brian Whitaker's article, "Conflict and catchphrases" in the *Guardian*, February 24, 2003, available at www.guardian.co.uk/world/2003/feb/24/worlddispatch.usa - accessed on December 5, 2008. The list of the Benador Associates clients is the who's who of the American neocon establishment, interlaced with the most publicly flaunted figures in the native informer category. "Readers who like to keep an eye on such things," Brian Whitaker concluded, "should watch out for media appearances

by any of the following Benador "experts": A.M. Rosenthal, Alexander M. Haig Jr, Amir Taheri, Arnaud de Borchgrave, Azar Nafisi, Barry Rubin, Charles Jacobs, Charles Krauthammer, Fereydoun Hoveyda, Frank J. Gaffney Jr, George Jonas, Hillel Fradkin, Ismail Cem, John Eibner, Kanan Makiya, Khalid Duran, Khidhir Hamza, Laurie Mylroie, Mansoor Ijaz, Martin Kramer, Max Boot, Meyrav Wurmser, Michael A. Ledeen, Michael Rubin, Michel Gurfinkiel, Paul Marshall, R. James Woolsey, Richard O. Spertzel, Richard Perle, Richard Pipes, Ruth Wedgwood, Shaykh Kabbani, Stanley H. Kaplan, Tashbih Sayyed, Tom Rose and Walid Phares."

34. For more details, see "Bestseller's lies exposed", *The Sydney Morning Herald*, July 24, 2004, at www.smh.com.au/articles/2004/07/23/1090464854793.html - accessed on 5 December 2008 - where you read the details of how: "Literary Editor Malcolm Knox uncovers Australia's latest hoax author. Her tragic story stole readers' hearts and triggered an international outcry. She became a best-selling author in the same league as J. K. Rowling and Michael Moore. She petitioned the United Nations personally, was published in 15 countries, and Australians voted her memoir into their favorite 100 books of all time. But Norma Khouri is a fake, and so is *Forbidden Love*."

35. For more on the post 9/11 modes of knowledge production, see my *Post-Orientalism: Knowledge and Power in Time of Terror* (New Brunswick, NJ: Transactions, 2008).

36. Alexis de Tocqueville, *Democracy in America*: 475.

37. There is nothing inherently colonial about any literature, including what is packaged as "Western literature", the best representatives of which have been read globally in liberating and emancipatory manners. I give examples of this manner of reading European and American (as well as Asian, African, and Latin American) literature in my *Iran: A People Interrupted* (New York: The New Press, 2007).

1   BROWN SKIN, WHITE MASKS

1.   Frantz Fanon, *Black Skin, White Masks*. Translated by Richard Philcox; with foreword by Kwame Anthony Appiah. (New York: Grove Press, 1952/2008): xi.

2.   Fanon, *Black Skin, White Masks*: xi–xiii.

3.   Fanon, *Black Skin, White Masks*: 2.

4.   Fanon, *Black Skin, White Masks*: 3.

5.   Fanon, *Black Skin, White Masks*: 2.

6.   Fanon, *Black Skin, White Masks*: 2–3.

7.   Fanon, *Black Skin, White Masks*: 3.

8.   Fanon, *Black Skin, White Masks*: 2.

9.   Fanon, *Black Skin, White Masks*: 4–5.

10. Fanon, *Black Skin, White Masks*: 9.

11. Fanon, *Black Skin, White Masks*: 15.

12. Fanon, *Black Skin, White Masks*: 18.

13. For an English translation, see Mayotte Capécia, *I Am a Martinican Woman & the White Negress: Two Novelettes* (Pueblo, CO: Passeggiata Press, 1998).

14. As quoted in Fanon, *Black Skin, White Masks*: 25.

15. Fanon, *Black Skin, White Masks*: 25.

16. Fanon, *Black Skin, White Masks*: 27.

17. Fanon, *Black Skin, White Masks*: 29–30.

18. Fanon, *Black Skin, White Masks*: 34.
19. Fanon, *Black Skin, White Masks*: 35, note 12. *Y a bon Banania* refers to the racist advertising images used to sell *Banania*, a popular chocolate drink in France. The term denotes a friendly but stupid African.
20. Fanon, *Black Skin, White Masks*: 35, note 12. Fanon subjects the Senegalese writer Abdoulaye Sadji's (1910–61) *Nini* to the same critical review.
21. See Derek Attridge's interview with Jacques Derrida, "This Strange Institution Called Literature", in his *Acts of Literature*, edited by Derek Attridge (London and New York: Routledge, 1992): 33–75.
22. Fanon, *Black Skin, White Masks*: 45.
23. For an English translation of the more famous novel of René Maran, see his *Batoula*. (New York: Heinemann International Literature & Textbooks, 1973).
24. Fanon, *Black Skin, White Masks*: 47.
25. Fanon, *Black Skin, White Masks*: 47.
26. Fanon, *Black Skin, White Masks*: 47.
27. Fanon, *Black Skin, White Masks*: 48.
28. Fanon, *Black Skin, White Masks*: 50.
29. Fanon, *Black Skin, White Masks*: 53.
30. Fanon, *Black Skin, White Masks*: 60–61.
31. Fanon, *Black Skin, White Masks*: 62–63.
32. Fanon, *Black Skin, White Masks*: 63.
33. Fanon, *Black Skin, White Masks*: 65.
34. Fanon, *Black Skin, White Masks*: 70.
35. See Anne Applebaum, "The Fight for Muslim Women", *Washington Post*, February 4, 2007, at www.washingtonpost.com/wp-dyn/content/article/2007/02/01/AR2007020102307.html—accessed on December 12, 2008. For even higher cascades of praise, see William Grimes, "No Rest for a Feminist Fighting Radical Islam", *New York Times*, February 14, 2007, available at www.nytimes.com/2007/02/14/books/14grim.html?_r=2&oref=slogin—accessed on December 15, 2008—where you will be told that is a "brave, inspiring and beautifully written memoir". The hypocrisy of Hirsi Ali's admirers in North America and Western Europe lies in the phrase "Radical Islam" in the title of William Grimes's review. Hirsi Ali's beef is not against radical Islam—it is against Islam.
36. For more on how Hirsi Ali lied about her past in order to get Dutch citizenship, which in turn resulted in her being expelled from the Dutch parliament, see Nicholas Watt, "MP in Immigration Row to Leave Netherlands: Somali-Born Politician Admits Lying to get Asylum", (*Guardian,* May 16, 2006), available at www.guardian.co.uk/world/2006/may/16/nicholaswatt.mainsection—accessed on December 14, 2008.
37. Soon after the release of *Submission* (2004), a rabidly anti-Islamic film by the late Dutch film-maker Theo Van Gogh and Hirsi Ali, they were widely accused of having plagiarized the Iranian artist Shirin Neshat. The Dutch journalist Francisco van Jole laid out the proof, noting that Shirin Neshat had exhibited her work in the Netherlands in 1997 and 2000. "Anyone who compares the images," he said, "automatically gets the taste of plagiarism in their mouth. The worst thing is that neither Hirsi Ali nor Van Gogh acknowledges the debt. As self-declared Muslim emancipators, they must be familiar with Shirin Neshat's work. The only reason I can think of to explain the concealment is that Shirin Neshat's message does not tally with their views." For more details, see "Hirsi

Ali and Van Gogh Deny Muslim Film is Plagiarism", in *E: Expatica*, September 1, 2004, at www.expatica.com—accessed December 14, 2008.
38. Fanon, *Black Skin, White Masks*: 71.
39. Fanon, *Black Skin, White Masks*: 71.
40. Fanon, *Black Skin, White Masks*: 71.
41. Fanon, *Black Skin, White Masks*: 88.
42. See his *The Foreigner's Gift: The Americans, the Arabs, and the Iraqis in Iraq* (New York: Free Press, 2007).
43. See *Cruelty and Silence: War, Tyranny, Uprising, and the Arab World* (New York: W. W. Norton, 1994) for his take on the Iraqi society before it was leveled in the invasion that he very much encouraged.
44. *Harper's*, September 2004.
45. For more on Hofstadter's groundbreaking observations on American political culture, see his *Anti-Intellectualism in American Life* (New York: Vintage, 1966).
46. See Niall Ferguson, *Colossus: The Price of America's Empire* (New York: Penguin, 2004).
47. See Irshad Manji's *The Trouble with Islam Today* (New York: St Martin Press, 2004). For an overarching critique of Gay International, see the groundbreaking work of Joseph Massad, *Desiring Arabs* (Chicago: University Chicago Press, 2007).

2 ON COMPRADOR INTELLECTUALS

1. See Russell Jacoby, *The Last Intellectuals: American Culture in the Age of Academe* (New York: Basic Books, 1987).
2. See Edward W. Said, *Representations of the Intellectual* (New York: Pantheon Books, 1994): 52–53.
3. See Kwame Anthony Appiah, *My Father's House: Africa in Philosophy of Culture* (London: Methuen, 1992): 149.
4. See www.famous-speeches-and-speech-topics.info/famous-speeches/malcolm-x-speech-message-to-the-grassroots.htm—accessed on September 12, 2010.
5. Albert Memmi, *The Colonizer and the Colonized* (Boston: Beacon Press, 1991): 15–16.
6. See www.famous-speeches-and-speech-topics.info/famous-speeches/malcolm-x-speech-message-to-the-grassroots.htm—accessed on September 12, 2010.
7. See Joseph Massad's "Political Realists or Comprador Intelligentsia: Palestinian Intellectuals and the National Struggle", *Critique*, Fall 1997: 21–35.
8. Massad "Political Realists or Comprador Intelligentsia": 23.
9. Massad "Political Realists or Comprador Intelligentsia": 32.
10. See Adam Shatz, "The Native Informant", *The Nation*, April 10, 2003.
11. See Ibn Warraq, *Why I Am Not a Muslim* (Portland: Prometheus Books, 1995).
12. See "Azar Nafisi: Author of *Reading Lolita in Tehran* converses with Robert Birnbaum". Posted: February 5, 2004. Available as of September 1, 2004 at www.identitytheory.com/interviews/birnbaum139.php.
13. Mark Lilla is today the picture perfect example of what the great American historian Richard Hofstadter (1916–70) thoroughly detected and analyzed more than half a century ago in his classic *Anti-Intellectualism in American Life* (New York: Vintage, 1966). The detection of this anti-intellectual streak in American culture goes back at least to Alex de Tocqueville early in the Nineteenth century.

14. See Mark Lilla, *The Reckless Mind: Intellectuals in Politics* (New York: New York Review Books, 2001): xi.
15. Mark Lilla, *The Reckless Mind*: 196.
16. Lilla, *The Reckless Mind*: 197.
17. Lilla, *The Reckless Mind*: 198.
18. Lilla, *The Reckless Mind*: 203–4.
19. See Lewis H. Lapham, "Notebook: *Dar al-Harb*", *Harper's*, March 2004: 9.
20. Lapham, "Notebook: *Dar al-Harb*": 8.
21. Lapham, "Notebook: *Dar al-Harb*": 7.
22. As reported by BBC News, "Blame widens for Abu Ghraib abuse", on August 26, 2004, and the *New York Times* of Friday August 27, 2004.
23. See Alan Dershowitz, "Is there a Torturous Road to Justice", *Los Angeles Times*, 8 November, 2001.
24. See Alan Dershowitz, "When All Else Fails, Why Not Torture", *American Legion Magazine*, July 2002.
25. The report of this interview was still on CBS website at the initial writing of this chapter on August 27, 2004. See www.cbsnews.com/ stories/2002/01/17/60minutes/main324751.shtml.
26. The text of this interview was still on CNN website at the initial writing of this chapter on August 27, 2004. See http://edition.cnn.com/2003/LAW/03/03/ cnna.Dershowitz/.
27. See Alan M. Dershowitz, *Why Terrorism Works* (New Haven, CT: Yale University Press, 2002).
28. See Michael Ignatieff, *The Lesser Evil: Political Ethics in an Age of Terror* (Princeton: Princeton University Press, 2004): 140.
29. Ignatieff, *The Lesser Evil: Political Ethics in an Age of Terror*: 143.
30. Ignatieff, *The Lesser Evil: Political Ethics in an Age of Terror*: 136.
31. Ignatieff, *The Lesser Evil: Political Ethics in an Age of Terror*: 138.
32. Ignatieff, *The Lesser Evil: Political Ethics in an Age of Terror*: 138.
33. Ignatieff, *The Lesser Evil: Political Ethics in an Age of Terror*: 137.
34. Ignatieff, *The Lesser Evil: Political Ethics in an Age of Terror*: 137.
35. Ignatieff, *The Lesser Evil: Political Ethics in an Age of Terror*: 139.
36. Ignatieff, *The Lesser Evil: Political Ethics in an Age of Terror*: 140.
37. Ignatieff, *The Lesser Evil: Political Ethics in an Age of Terror*: 140.
38. Ignatieff, *The Lesser Evil: Political Ethics in an Age of Terror*: 140.
39. Ignatieff, *The Lesser Evil: Political Ethics in an Age of Terror*: 142.
40. Ignatieff, *The Lesser Evil: Political Ethics in an Age of Terror*: 141.
41. Ignatieff, *The Lesser Evil: Political Ethics in an Age of Terror*: 141.
42. Ignatieff, *The Lesser Evil: Political Ethics in an Age of Terror*: 142.
43. Ignatieff, *The Lesser Evil: Political Ethics in an Age of Terror*: 142.
44. Ignatieff, *The Lesser Evil: Political Ethics in an Age of Terror*: 142.
45. Ignatieff, *The Lesser Evil: Political Ethics in an Age of Terror*: 142.
46. Ignatieff, *The Lesser Evil: Political Ethics in an Age of Terror*: 143.
47. Ignatieff, *The Lesser Evil: Political Ethics in an Age of Terror*: 144.
48. See Georg Simmel, *Conflict & The Web Of Group Affiliations* (New York: The Free Press, 1964).
49. See William Kornhauser, *The Politics of Mass Society* (New York: 1959): 184–5.
50. Kornhauser, *The Politics of Mass Society*: 185.
51. Kornhauser, *The Politics of Mass Society*: 187.

52. See Theodor Geiger, *Aufgaben und Stellung der Intelligentz in der Gesellschaft* (Stuttgart: Ferdinand Enke Verlag, 1949), as quoted in Kornhauser, *The Politics of Mass Society*: 187; footnote 8.
53. For more details on this see the chart Students and scholars (2001 estimates) in Lewis H. Lapham's "Tentacles of Rage: The Republican Propaganda Mill, A Brief History", *Harper's*, September 2004: 39.
54. See Ali al-Nezami al-Aruzi al-Samarqandi, *Kuliyyat Chahar Maqaleh*. Edited with an Introduction by Muhammad Abd al-Wahab Qazvini (Leiden: Brill, 1909): 26–53.

3   LITERATURE AND EMPIRE

1. There are, however, emerging signs of legal discrimination against Muslim women in the US, too, such as the case of Lisa Valentine in Douglasville, Georgia (near Atlanta), who was arrested and jailed for refusing to take off her headscarf at a courthouse security checkpoint. For more details, see "US judge jails Muslim woman over head scarf", *The Malaysian Insider*, December 19, 2008, available at www.themalaysianinsider.com/index.php/world/14408-us-judge-jails-muslim-woman-over-head-scarf - accessed on December 18, 2008.
2. See Seymour Hersh, "Annals of National Security: The Iran Plans", *New Yorker*, April 17, 2006.
3. See Niall Ferguson, *Colossus: The Price of American Empire* (London: Penguin, 2004): Chapter One.
4. See Michael Hardt and Antonio Negri *Empire* (Cambridge, MA: Harvard University Press, 2000).
5. V. G. Kiernan, *America, The New Imperialism: From White Settlement to World Hegemony* (London: Verso, 1978): xvi.
6. See Chalmers Johnson's Blowback Trilogy that includes *The Sorrows of Empire: Militarism, Secrecy, and the End of Republic* (New York: Holt Paperbacks, 2004).
7. I have covered this extensive literature on American empire, which mostly appeared in the aftermath of 9/11, in my "American Empire: Triumph of Triumphalism", *Unbound: Harvard Journal of the Legal Left*, Vol. 4, No. 82, 2008.
8. See Gayatri Chakravorty Spivak, "Can the Subaltern Speak?" in Cary Nelson and Lawrence Grossberg (eds), *Marxism and Interpretation of Culture* (Chicago: University of Illinois Press, 1988): 297. For a pioneering critic of the abuse of Muslim women's rights in Bush's war of terrorism, see Miriam Cooke, "Islamic Feminism before and after September 11", *Duke Journal of Gender Law and Policy*, Vol. 9: 227, 2003.
9. See Betty Mahmoody and William Hoffer, *Not without my Daughter* (New York: St Martin Press, 1991). This book was later turned into a movie. There are also reports that *Reading Lolita in Tehran* is being turned into a movie.
10. For the full text of Thomas Macaulay's speech see Lynn Zastoupil and Martin Moir (eds), *The Great Indian Education Debate: Documents Relating to the Orientalist-Anglicist Debate 1781–1843* (London: Routledge, 2000): 171. After this general injunction Macaulay adds: "To that class we may leave it to refine the vernacular dialects of this country... " That would be the White Man's burden, carried, like the rest of his luggage on his colonial conquest, by a native, though this time by a *native informer*.

11. In her Acknowledgements Nafisi thanks Paul Wolfowitz for giving her Leo
Strauss's *Persecution and the Art of Writing* to read. After the initial publication
of this chapter as an essay in *Al-Ahram* and following the scandal of Paul
Wolfowitz both as the US Deputy Secretary of Defense under George W.
Bush and later his corrupt leadership of the World Bank, Nafisi began denying that
the Paul in her Acknowledgements is Wolfowitz, and her supporters echoed that
denial. For the text of her denial see her email to Doug Ireland and Danny Postel:
"Without being coy I reserve my right to keep the identity of Paul private and
not let my relationships become political inferences either in support or against
certain views." (As posted on Doug Ireland's weblog at http://direland.typepad.
com/direland/2004/10/azar_nafisi_rep.html—accessed on September 12, 2010).
There are two very clear reasons that the Paul she thanks is Wolfowitz—
one external and the other internal to the text. Nafisi's supporter Christopher
Hitchens wrote a laudatory essay comparing her to Czeslaw Milosz, in which
he revealed that this Paul is indeed Wolfowitz (See Christopher Hitchens, "The
Captive Mind Now", *Slate*, August 330, 2004). More important, Nafisi thanks
"Paul" for introducing her to *Persecution and the Art of Writing*, which she fails
to mention is by the guru of the entire neocon cabal, Leo Strauss. On the link
between Strauss and Wolfowitz (among other neocons), see Anne Norton's *Leo
Strauss and the Politics of American Empire* (New Haven, CT: Yale University
Press, 2004).

12. See Edward W. Said *Culture and Imperialism* (New York: Vintage, 1993).

13. See Amy Kaplan *The Anarchy of Empire in the Making of US Culture*
(Cambridge, MA: Harvard University Press, 2002).

14. See Gauri Viswanathan's *Masks of Conquest: Literary Study and British Rule
in India* (New York: Columbia University Press, 1989).

15. Here it is crucial to keep in mind that the white racist intellectual is not quite
happy to see his colored counterparts assuming center stage in the heart of
the empire—either those who serve it or those who oppose it. To him they are
the same. Among the silliest pieces written on my essay on *Reading Lolita in
Tehran* soon after it appeared at *Al-Ahram* in summer 2006 was one by a certain
Gideon Lewis-Kraus ("Pawn of the Neocons? The Debate over *Reading Lolita
in Tehran*", *Slate*, November 30, 2006). "In the end," this person concluded,
"Dabashi must conspire with Nafisi to make the book more important that [sic]
it is: The besieged Nafisi gets to preserve her fantasy that removing her veil to
read Austen in her home was not only therapeutically powerful but politically
noble, and Dabashi gets to preserve his fantasy that criticizing Nafisi makes
him a usefully engaged intellectual. But those whose fingers are on the triggers
of those targeted nuclear warheads couldn't possibly care about what either of
them has to say." To critics such as Lewis-Kraus, the only reason that a colored
person might utter a word of protest is to get recognition that he is "a usefully
engaged intellectual"—for they lack the faintest idea of a principled position and
a moral stand on anything. Everything for them is a call for recognition. What his
barely concealed racism betrays, though, dismissing two colored "intellectuals"
who have for a moment stolen from him the center stage, is how his "those
whose fingers are on triggers" stands really for him—the racist intellectual, the
arbiter of truth, the White Man with his finger on nuclear triggers, momentarily
inconvenienced by two colored characters walking on his stage.

16. Roland Barthes, "The Photographic Message", in *A Barthes Reader* (New
York: Hills and Wang, 1982): 195–8. For a comparison of the cover of *Reading*

Lolita in Tehran and the original photo from which it was cropped, see my "Native Informers and the Making of the American Empire", *Al-Ahram*, June 1–7, 2006, from which this chapter is excerpted.

17. See Malek Alloula's *The Colonial Harem* (Minneapolis, MN: University of Minnesota Press, 1986).

18. For more details on the publishing history of Nabokov's *Lolita* see Jeff Edmunds, "'Lolita': Complex, often tricky and 'a hard sell'", CNN, April 9, 1999), at www.cnn.com/SPECIALS/books/1999/nabokov/lolita.sociological.essay/— accessed on December 20, 2008. The dubious distinction of "the filthiest book I have ever read" has been given to other books as well. Magistrate Andrew Macrery called Frank Harris's "My Life and Loves" the same thing. (See *International Herald Tribune*, December 1, 2000).

4   THE HOUSE MUSLIM

1. See David Damrosch, *What is World Literature* (Princeton, NJ: Princeton University Press, 2003) 283–4.

2. See Edward Said's *The World, the Text, and the Critic* (Cambridge, MA: Harvard University Press, 1983); and Gayatri Chakravorty Spivak's *Death of a Discipline* (New York, NY: Columbia University Press, 2005) for details of these two concepts.

3. For more on my take on American triumphant nativism, see my essay, "American Empire: The Triumph of Triumphalism", *Unbound: Harvard Journal of the Legal Left*, Vol. 4; 82, 2008.

4. *The Wall Street Journal*, September 29, 2003.

5. For a short account of the terror coming my way in response to my speaking and writing against the terror that the US and Israel are inflicting on innocent people, see my "Forget the Reds under the Bed, there are Arabs in the Attic", *Times Higher Education Supplement*, October 17, 2003. The longer description of the attacks on any one who dares telling the American emperor that his pants are on fire or that Israel is a racist apartheid state is too nauseating to tell. The perpetrators of the terror themselves are quite proud of their deeds and provide ample evidence of their McCarthyite practices. See, for example, David Horowitz, *The Professors: The 101 Most Dangerous Academics in America* (Washington, DC: Regnery, 2007).

6. From an interview with *The Religion Report: Radio National*, dated October 10, 2001, see www.abc.net.au/rn/talks/8.30/relrpt/stories/s386913.htm—accessed on December 24, 2008.

7. I have seen five such books: Ibn Warraq, *Why I Am Not a Muslim* (Portland, OR: Prometheus Books, 1995); Ibn Warraq, *The Origin of the Koran: Classics Essays on Islam's Holy Book* (Portland, OR: Prometheus Books, 1998); Ibn Warraq (ed.), *The Quest for the Historical Muhammad* (Portland, OR: Prometheus Books, 2000); Ibn Warraq (ed.), *What the Koran Really Says: Language, Text, and Commentary* (Portland: Prometheus Books, 2002); Ibn Warraq (ed.), *Leaving Islam: Apostates Speak Out* (Portland, OR: Prometheus Books, 2003). But essays, articles, and interviews by and with Ibn Warraq have grown exponentially, positing the probability that there could be more than one Ibn Warraq.

8. For example, see Jamie Glazov's "Defending the West", *FrontPage Magazine. com*, December 24, 2008, at www.frontpagemag.com/Articles/Read.

aspx?GUID=2A18D144-3030-41EF-A28B-2695E2A68617—accessed on December 24, 2008.

9. From an interview with *The Religion Report*, Radio National, dated October 10, 2001. See www.abc.net.au/rn/talks/8.30/relrpt/stories/s386913.htm—accessed December 24, 2008.

10. *The Religion Report*: Radio National.

11. *The Wall Street Journal*, September 29, 2003. Ibn Warraq has now fully developed his hatred of Edward Said into a full fledged volume, *Defending the West: A Critique of Edward Said's Orientalism* (Portland, OR: Prometheus Books, 2007).

12. *The Wall Street Journal*, September 29, 2003.

13. This active personification of self-hatred, staged publicly, may have just assumed new proportions in Azar Nafisi's second memoir, *Things I've Been Silent About: Memories* (New York: Random House, 2008), in which, according to her publisher, she has evidently mixed her autobiographical recollection of her domineering and delusional mother and that of the Islamic Republic into an intertwined narrative. Her decision, we are told by her publisher, to divulge her family secrets is integral to her outspoken disposition against the Islamic Republic. This book should make for a fascinating read as a study in self-loathing and should bring Nafisi closer to Ibn Warraq and Hirsi Ali in their common pathologies.

14. Ibn Warraq, *Why I Am Not a Muslim*: xiii.

15. Ibn Warraq, *Why I Am Not a Muslim*: xv.

16. Ibn Warraq, *Why I Am Not a Muslim*: 1.

17. Ibn Warraq, *Why I Am Not a Muslim*: 2.

18. By "stupidity" I do not mean an insult but a diagnosis, taking my clue from the excellent argument of Thomas H. Benton in his column, "On Stupidity", *The Chronicle of Higher Education*, August 1, 2008. Here is his opening argument, paving the way for the audience on which Ibn Warraq can count: "No one ever went broke underestimating the intelligence of the American public," said H.L. Mencken in the era of *Babbitt* and the Scopes "Monkey Trial". Several generations later, one might speculate that no publisher has ever lost money with a book accusing Americans—particularly young ones—of being stupid. The most influential book in that genre is surely Richard Hofstadter's *Anti-Intellectualism in American Life* (1963), in which he argues that the American dislike for educational elitism derives from a number of interlocking cultural legacies, including religious fundamentalism, populism, the privileging of "common sense" over esoteric knowledge, the pragmatic values of business and science, and the cult of the self-made man. With some cyclical variation, Americans tend to distrust, resent, and even feel moral revulsion toward "intellectuals".

19. Ibn Warraq, *The Origins of the Koran (1998)*: 9.

20. For more detail, see my chapter on Goldziher in my *Post-Orientalism: Knowledge and Power in Time of Terror*.

21. For more details, see Max Scheler's *Problems of a Sociology of Knowledge* (London: Routledge and Kegan Paul, 1980); and Karl Mannheim's *Ideology and Utopia* (New York: Harcourt, Brace, 1936), as well as Karl Mannheim's *Essays on the Sociology of Knowledge* (New York: Oxford University Press, 1952).

22. For a single volume collection of the most influential writings on sociology of knowledge, see Gunter W. Remmling (ed.), *Towards the Sociology of*

Knowledge: Origin and Development of a Sociological Thought Style (New York: Humanities Press, 1973).

23. See Tom W. Goff, *Marx and Mead: Contributions to Sociology of Knowledge* (London: Routledge and Kegan Paul, 1980).

24. For a collection of classical essays on *Verstehendemethode*, including Weber's, see Marcello Truzzi (ed.), *Verstehen: Subjective Understanding in the Social Sciences* (London: Addison-Wesley Publishing Company, 1974).

25. See Hans-Georg Gadamer's *Truth and Method* (New York: Crossroad, 1975).

26. Michel Foucault, *Discipline and Punish: The Birth of the Prison* (New York: Pantheon Books, 1977): 203.

27. For the most recent futile attempt at restoring legitimacy to the bankrupt Orientalist project, see Robert Irwin's *Dangerous Knowledge: Orientalism and Its Discontents* (New York: Overlook, 2006).

28. See "Massive Israeli air raid on Gaza", *BBC News*, December 27, 2008, available at http://news.bbc.co.uk/2/hi/middle_east/7800985.stm—accessed on December 27, 2008.

29. See *New York Times*, December 27, 2008, at www.nytimes.com/2008/12/28/world/middleast/28mideast.html?_r=1&hp—accessed on December 27, 2008.

30. See "UN official slams Israel 'crimes'", *BBC News*, December 10, 2008, at http://news.bbc.co.uk/2/hi/middle_east/7774988.stm—accessed on December 31, 2008: "The UN special rapporteur on human rights in the Palestinian territories has said Israel's policies there amount to a crime against humanity. Richard Falk's statement came as UN human rights delegates urged Israel to take nearly 100 measures including ending its blockade of the Gaza Strip."

31. See "Obama's Gaza silence condemned", *Aljazeera*, December 31, 2008, at http://english.aljazeera.net/news/americas/2008/12/2008123101532604810.html—accessed on December 31, 2008.

32. See *Ha"aretz* front page on December 28, 2008 at www.haaretz.com—accessed on December 28, 2008. Buried in the bottom of the page was the courageous Isareli journalist Amira Haas's report, "'Little Baghdad' in Gaza—bombs, fear, and rage", in which she began her piece by reporting: "There are many corpses and wounded, every moment another casualty is added to the list of the dead, and there is no more room in the morgue. Relatives search among the bodies and the wounded in order to bring the dead quickly to burial. A mother whose three school-age children were killed, and are piled one on top of the other in the morgue, screams and then cries, screams again and then is silent." Amira Haas and a handful of other Israelis are safeguarding the Jewish soul that must survive this carnage they call "Israel" for posterity.

33. See "Massive Israeli air raid on Gaza", *BBC News*, December 27, 2008, available at http://news.bbc.co.uk/2/hi/middle_east/7800985.stm—accessed on December 27, 2008.

34. See "Israel launches fierce air strikes on Gaza", *Financial Times*, December 27, 2008, available at www.ft.com/world—accessed on December 27, 2008.

35. Just received (New Year's Eve 2008/09) an email from a human rights activist from Palestine. He writes: "So far hundreds of civilians have been killed in Gaza. Five sisters in one family, four other children in another home, two children on a cart drawn by a donkey. Universities, colleges, police stations, roads, apartment buildings were all targeted ..."

36. Ibn Warraq, *The Quest for the Historical Muhammad* (2000): 78.

37. See Jaroslav Pelikan, *Jesus Through the Centuries: His Place in the History of Culture* (New Haven: Yale University Press, 1999).

38. Annemarie Schimmel has done a fine study of the significance of Muhammad in Muslim piety through the ages. See her *And Muhammad Is His Messenger: The Veneration of the Prophet in Islamic Piety* (Chapel Hill, NC: The University of North Carolina Press, 1985).

39. Ibn Warraq, *What the Koran Really Says* (2002): 23.

40. See "FBI records detail Koran claims", *BBC News*, May 26, 2005. Available at http://news.bbc.co.uk/2/hi/americas/4581383.stm—accessed on December 31, 2008: "An inmate at the Guantanamo Bay prison camp accused US guards of flushing a Koran down the toilet in 2002, newly declassified FBI documents reveal."

41. Ibn Warraq, *Leaving Islam* (2003).

42. Ibn Warraq, *Leaving Islam*: 138.

43. Ibn Warraq, *Leaving Islam*: 169.

44. Ibn Warraq, *Leaving Islam*: 201.

45. Ibn Warraq, *Leaving Islam*: 400.

46. Ibn Warraq, *Leaving Islam*: 400.

47. As reported by BBC on May 21, 2004 on their website. Available at http://news.bbc.co.uk/1/hi/world/americas/3734531.stm—accessed on December 28, 2008.

48. Malcolm X, "Message To The Grass Roots", delivered on November 10, 1963. Available at www.americanrhetoric.com/speeches/malcolmxgrassroots.htm—accessed on December 28, 2008.

CONCLUSION

1. That violence is integral to all politics, but that the contemporary militant adventurism of Osama bin Laden and company lack any political, social, or economic program that qualifies them as such, is the subject of my book *Islamic Liberation Theology: Resisting the Empire* (London: Routledge, 2008).

2. For more on Congressman Emanuel's background see "Profile: Rahm Emanuel", *BBC News*, November 7, 2008), available at http://news.bbc.co.uk/2/hi/americas/7702408.stm—accessed on January 14, 2009. For more details on the history of ethnic cleansing in Palestine, see Ilan Pappe, *The Ethnic Cleansing of Palestine* (London: Oneworld Publications, 2007).

3. For more details, see "Obama pledges support for Israel", *BBC News*, June 4, 2008), available at http://news.bbc.co.uk/2/hi/americas/7435883.stm—accessed on January 15, 2009.

4. For more background on Obama's appointment of Emanuel as his chief of staff, see Ali Abunimah, "Obama picks pro-Israel hardliner for top post", *Electronic Intifada*, November 5, 2008—available at http://electronicintifada.net/v2/article9939.shtml—accessed on January 12, 2009.

5. For more details of this interview, see "Emanuel to be Obama's chief of staff", *Jerusalem Post Online*, November 6, 2008, available at www.jpost.com/servlet/Satellite?cid=1225910047157&pagename=JPost%2FJPArticle%2FPrinter—accessed on January 12, 2009.

6. For more details, see "Rahm Emanuel apologizes for father's disparaging remarks about Arabs", *Ha'aretz*, November 17, 2008, available at www.

haaretz.com/hasen/spages/1037256.html—accessed on January 12, 2009. "From the fullness of my heart," Emanuel was quoted as saying to a representative of the American-Arab Anti-Discrimination Committee, "I personally apologize on behalf of my family and me. These are not the values upon which I was raised or those of my family."

7. For a representative sample see the following report in Ha'aretz: "'Mohammed's a pig', 'Death to Arabs' sprayed on Jaffa mosque", Ha'aretz, December 21, 2008, available at www.haaretz.com/hasen/spages/1048562.html—accessed on December 21, 2008.

8. "Israelis were the only people in the world who hoped the Republican candidate would win." This according to the Israeli columnist Akiva Eldar, writing for Ha'aretz, now pleading with Obama after his election not to "let the Israelis bleed and kill all the way to an ostracized apartheid state." See Akiva Eldar, "Obama's Choice: Truman or Marshall", Ha'aretz, January 19, 2009), available at www.haaretz.com/hasen/spages/1056660.html—accessed on January 19, 2009.

9. For more details on this mantra, see the text of the foreign policy speech Senator John McCain gave at the Los Angeles World Affairs Council, "John McCain's Foreign Policy Speech", New York Times, March 26, 2008), available atwww.nytimes.com/glogin?URI=http://www.nytimes.com/2008/03/26/us/politics/26text-mccain.html—accessed on January 14, 2009.

10. For the full text of Obama and McCain's speech see "Obama, McCain comedy riffs; Obama middle name really "Steve" Transcripts", Chicago Sun-Times, October 16, 2008, available at http://blogs.suntimes.com/sweet/2008/10/obama_comedy_rift_middle_name.html—accessed on January 14, 2009.

11. The incident is something to be seen and heard, rather than just read. Its video is available on YouTube, at www.youtube.com/watch?v=0YIq5Q15L1o&feature=related—accessed on January 12, 2009.

12. Obama has given detailed account of his winding way towards his identity formations in his Dreams from My Father: A Story of Race and Inheritance (New York, Canongate, 1995).

13. See Richard Cohen, "Obama's Farrakhan Test", Washington Post, January 15, 2008, available atwww.washingtonpost.com/wp-dyn/content/article/2008/01/14/AR2008011402083.html—accessed on January 14, 2009.

14. Barack Obama had started distancing himself from Reverend Wright as early as February 10, 2007, the day he announced his candidacy for presidency, when he initially invited and then disinvited Reverend Wright to deliver a public invocation. See "Disinvitation by Obama is Criticized", New York Times, March 6, 2007, available at www.nytimes.com/2007/03/06/us/politics/06obama.html—accessed on January 14, 2009.

15. For a fuller discussion of Islamic liberation theology and it affinities with Christian liberation theology, see my Islamic Liberation Theology: Resisting the Empire.

16. For a detailed discussion of the "charges" of being a Muslim leveled against Obama, see Perry Bacon, Jr "Foes Use Obama's Muslim Ties to Fuel Rumors About Him", Washington Post, November 29, 2007, available at www.washingtonpost.com/wp-dyn/content/article/2007/11/28/AR2007112802757.html?hpid=topnews—accessed on January 15, 2009. "In his speeches and often on the internet," Perry Bacon Jr wrote, "the part of Sen. Barack Obama's

biography that gets the most attention is not his race but his connections to the Muslim world. Since declaring his candidacy for president in February, Obama, a member of a congregation of the United Church of Christ in Chicago, has had to address assertions that he is a Muslim or that he had received training in Islam in Indonesia, where he lived from ages six to ten. While his father was an atheist and his mother did not practise religion, Obama's stepfather did occasionally attend services at a mosque there."

17. See Edward N. Luttwak, "President Apostate?" *New York Times*, May 1, 2008, available at www.nytimes.com/2008/05/12/opinion/12luttwak.html—accessed on January 13, 2009.

18. The Huffington Post May 23, 2008, available at www.huffingtonpost. com/2008/05/23/clinton-kennedy-assassina_n_103319.html—accessed on January 13, 2009.

19. Edward N. Luttwak, "President Apostate?"

20. Edward Nicolae Luttwak seems to be an expert on military coups as well as a scholar of Islamic law. See his *Coup d'état: A Practical Handbook* (Cambridge, MA: Harvard University Press, 2006).

21. See Clark Hoyt, "Entitled to Their Opinions, Yes. But Their Facts?", *New York Times*, June 1, 2008, available at www.nytimes.com/2008/06/01/opinion/01pubed.html?_r=1&oref=slogin—accessed on January 13, 2009.

22. For the original cover of the *New Yorker* magazine, see *The New Yorker*, July 21, 2008; and for more on this cover controversy see "Yikes! Controversial *New Yorker* Cover Shows Muslim, Flag-Burning, Osama-Loving, Fist-Bumping Obama", *Huffington Post*, July 13, 2008, available at www.huffingtonpost. com/2008/07/13/yikes-controversial-emnew_n_112429.html—accessed on January 13, 2009.

23. For more details, see "CNN apology over Obama name slip", *BBC News*, January 4, 2007, available at: http://news.bbc.co.uk/2/hi/americas/6229649. stm—accessed on January 13, 2009. The irony, of course, is that Obama's first name, Barack, from Arabic, sounds identical to Wolf Blitzer's last name in Hebrew, Ze'ev Barak, under which name he used to write for Israeli and American Israel Public Affairs Committee ooutlets. When Rahm Emanuel was appointed as Barack Obama's chief of staff, Wolf Blitzer made a point about the middle name of Rahm Emanuel, "Israel," and the middle name of Barack Obama, "Hussein"—adding that "only in America can a Hussein and an Israel be in the White House".

24. See "Barack Obama plans to reach out to Muslim world", *Chicago Tribune*, December 9, 2008, available at www.chicagotribune.com/news/politics/obama/chi-barack-obama-muslim-1210,0,5694976.story?page=1—accessed on January 15, 2009. Later reports indicated that Obama may have changed his mind. According to a column in the *Washington Post* by Mary Ann Akers, "The joint committee today [December 17, 2008] released the full schedule of Obama's Jan. 20 swearing-in ceremonies, which aides say is due to go to print this week. The schedule refers to the president-elect throughout the program as "Barack H. Obama" not "Barack Hussein Obama"." See Mary Ann Akers, "I Barack Hussein Obama Do Solemnly Swear...", *Washington Post*, December 17, 2008, available at http://voices.washingtonpost.com/sleuth/2008/12/president-elect_obama_has_said.html—accessed on January 15, 2009.

25. For the details of this encounter of Obama with members of this Florida synagogue, see "Obama Seeks Jewish Support in Florida Trip", NPR, May 23, 2008, available at www.npr.org/templates/transcript/transcript. php?storyId=90755741—accessed on January 15, 2009.

26. See Michael Eric Dyson, "His Way With Words Begins at the Pulpit", *Washington Post*, January 18, 2009, available at www.washingtonpost.com/wp-dyn/content/article/2009/01/16/AR2009011602312.html?hpid=opinionsbox1—accessed on January 18, 2009.

27. See Michael Eric Dyson, "His Way With Words Begins at the Pulpit". For more on the manner in which Obama mimics Malcolm X's speech patterns and other demeanors, see my "Limits of Obama's Imagination", *Al-Ahram*, February 21–27, 2008, as well as my "Obama's Palestinian problem", *Al-Ahram*, June 26–July 2, 2008, and "I, Barack Hussein Obama" ... *Al-Ahram*, November 13–19, 2008).

28. I have made this argument in extensive detail in my *Islamic Liberation Theology: Resisting the Empire*.

29. See Jennifer Peltz, "Madoff Case Sparks Anti-Semitism Fears: Madoff scandal fits profile of 'affinity fraud', proves particularly wrenching for Jews", *Associated Press*, New York, reported by *ABC News* on December 25, 2008, available at http://abcnews.go.com/Business/wireStory?id=6528133—accessed on 26 December 2008.

30. Jennifer Peltz, "Madoff Case Sparks Anti-Semitism Fears: Madoff scandal fits profile of 'affinity fraud', proves particularly wrenching for Jews".

31. Jennifer Peltz, "Madoff Case Sparks Anti-Semitism Fears: Madoff scandal fits profile of 'affinity fraud', proves particularly wrenching for Jews".

32. Jennifer Peltz, "Madoff Case Sparks Anti-Semitism Fears: Madoff scandal fits profile of 'affinity fraud', proves particularly wrenching for Jews".

33. See "India tops migrant workers table",(*BBC News*, March 19, 2008, available at http://news.bbc.co.uk/2/hi/business/7305667.stm—accessed on January 17, 2009. The global figure of immigrant workers has gone from 75 million in 1965 to 130 million in 2000, to almost 300 million by 2008, producing a "total global remittances in 2007 ... estimated by the World Bank to be \$318bn of which \$240bn went to people in developing countries", according to this report.

34. Gayatri Chakravorty Spivak, *Imperative zur Neuerfindung des Planeten/ Imperative to Re-Imagine the Planet* (Wien: Passagen Verlag, 1999): 38.

35. Spivak, *Imperative zur Neuerfindung des Planeten/Imperative to Re-Imagine the Planet*: 40.

36. Spivak, *Imperative zur Neuerfindung des Planeten/Imperative to re-Imagine the Planet*: 44.

37. Spivak, *Imperative zur Neuerfindung des Planeten/Imperative to re-Imagine the Planet*: 44–46.

38. A Danish television crew has done a short piece on young Israelis going for a picnic on their southern border and watching their army slaughtering Palestinians in Gaza, while having cappuccino and other goodies. You can watch the documentary here: www.youtube.com/watch?v=Tjw8U0AcH4Q—accessed on January 19, 2009.

39. See Thomas Friedman, "Israel's Goals in Gaza?", *New York Times*, January 13, 2009, available at http://www.nytimes.com/2009/01/14/opinion/14friedman.html—accessed on January 17, 2009.

40. See "Nine Arrested In Pro-Palestinian Rally In New York", *All Headline News*, January 12, 2009, available at http://www.allheadlinenews.com/articles/7013676352—accessed on January 17, 2009.
41. See "Nine Arrested In Pro-Palestinian Rally In New York": "A counter-demonstration was held by thousands of supporters of Israel outside the Israeli Consulate in New York. The rally sponsored by the United Jewish Communities Federation of New York and the Jewish Community Relations Council of New York was attended by New York Gov. David Paterson and U.S. Sen. Charles Schumer (D-NY), according to the Jewish Telegraphic Agency."

Index

Compiled by Sue Carlton

Milton Keynes UK
Ingram Content Group UK Ltd.
UKHW032102081124
450761UK00003B/57